Certificate BA2

FUNDAMENTALS OF MANAGEMENT ACCOUNTING

For exams from 2023

Exam Practice Kit

In this edition

- Banks of objective test questions covering the whole syllabus
- Answers with detailed feedback
- Advice on exam technique

First edition 2016
Seventh edition 2022

ISBN 9781 0355 0273 8
Previous ISBN 9781 5097 4038 3
eISBN 9781 0355 0324 7

British Library Cataloguing-in-Publication Data
A catalogue record for this book is available from the British Library

Published by

BPP Learning Media Ltd
BPP House, Aldine Place
142–144 Uxbridge Road
London W12 8AA

www.bpp.com/learningmedia

Printed in the United Kingdom

Your learning materials, published by BPP Learning Media Ltd, are printed on paper obtained from traceable sustainable sources.

We are grateful to the Chartered Institute of Management Accountants for permission to reproduce past examination questions. The suggested solutions in the exam answer bank have been prepared by BPP Learning Media Ltd.

Contents

Question and Answer index

BPP LEARNING MEDIA

Using your BPP Exam Practice Kit

One of the key criteria for achieving exam success is question practice. There is generally a direct correlation between candidates who study all topics and practise exam questions and those who are successful in their exams. This Kit gives you ample opportunity for such practice throughout your preparations for your OT exam.

All questions in your exam are compulsory and all the component learning outcomes will be examined so you must **study the whole syllabus**. Selective studying will limit the number of questions you can answer and hence reduce your chances of passing.

Practising as many exam-style questions as possible will be the key to passing this exam. You must do questions under **timed conditions** as part of your preparations.

Breadth of question coverage

Questions will cover the whole of the syllabus so you must study all the topics in the syllabus.

The weightings in the table below indicate the approximate proportion of study time you should spend on each topic, and is related to the number of questions per syllabus area in the exam.

BA2: Fundamentals of Management Accounting	
Syllabus topics	Weighting
A The Context of Management Accounting	10%
B Costing	25%
C Planning and Control	30%
D Decision Making	35%

Errata

BPP Learning Media do everything possible to ensure the material is accurate and up to date when sending to print. In the event that any errors are found after the print date, they are uploaded to the following website: https://learningmedia.bpp.com/catalog?pagename=Errata

The Exam

The exam is a computer based assessment, which is available on demand at assessment centres all year round.

The exams at Certificate Level can be taken in any order, but candidates must pass or be exempt from them all before they can move on to the Operational Level.

Each exam lasts for two hours and will contain 60 questions.

The exam will be made up of different types of questions, as shown below:

Question Type	Explanation
Multiple choice	Standard multiple choice items provide four options. One option is correct and the other three are incorrect. Incorrect options will be plausible, so you should expect to have to use detailed, syllabus-specific knowledge to identify the correct answer rather than relying on common sense.
Multiple response	A multiple response item is the same as a multiple choice question, except more than one response is required. You will be told how many options you need to select.
Number entry	Number entry (or 'fill in the blank') questions require you to type a short numerical response. You should carefully follow the instructions in the question in terms of how to type your answer – eg the correct number of decimal places.
Drag and drop	Drag and drop questions require you to drag a 'token' onto a pre-defined area. These tokens can be images or text. This type of question is effective at testing the order of events, labelling a diagram or linking events to outcomes.
Hot spot	These questions require you to identify an area or location on an image by clicking on it. This is commonly used to identify a specific point on a graph or diagram.
Item set	Two to four questions all relating to the same short scenario. Each question will be 'standalone', such that your ability to answer subsequent questions in the set does not rely on getting the first one correct.

Passing the exam

- Read, and **re-read the question** to ensure you fully understand what is being asked.

- When starting to read a question, especially one with a lengthy scenario, **read the requirement first**. You will then find yourself considering the requirement as you read the data in the scenario, helping you to focus on exactly what you have to do.

- **Do not spend too much time on one question** – remember you should spend two minutes, on average, per question.

- If you cannot decide between two answers – look carefully and decide whether for one of the options you are making an unnecessary assumption – **do not be afraid of trusting your gut instinct.**

- **Do not keep changing your mind** – research has shown that the first answer that appeals to you is often the correct one.

- Remember that marks are awarded for correct answers, and marks will not be deducted for incorrect answers. Therefore **answer every single question**, even ones you are unsure of.

- Always submit an answer for a given question even if you do not know the answer – **never leave any answers blank**.

- **Pace yourself** – you will need to work through the exam at the right speed. Too fast and your accuracy may suffer, too slow and you may run out of time. Use this Kit to practise your time keeping and approach to answering each question.

- If you are unsure about anything, remember to **ask the test administrator** before the test begins.

- Remember to **keep moving on!** You may be presented with a question which you simply cannot answer due to difficulty or if the wording is too vague. If you find yourself spending five minutes determining the answer for a question then your time management skills are poor and you are wasting valuable time.

- If you finish the exam with time to spare, use the rest of the time to **review your answers** and to make sure that you answered every question.

Questions

1 Introduction to management accounting

1   Which of the following is NOT part of the CIMA definition of management accounting?

    ○   Having skills, knowledge and expertise
    ○   Determining capital structure and funding that structure
    ○   Informing operational decisions
    ○   Planning long, medium and short run operations

2   Which of the following is NOT part of the role of CIMA?

    ○   Offering a continuing education scheme to its members
    ○   Ensuring that each member complies with CIMA's regulations
    ○   Issuing a code of ethics
    ○   Upholding public confidence in management accounting

3   What is the purpose of management information?

    ○   Planning only
    ○   Planning and control only
    ○   Planning, control and decision making only
    ○   Planning, control, decision making and research and development

4   For whom are management accounts prepared?

    ○   Employees
    ○   Internal managers
    ○   Shareholders
    ○   Suppliers

5   CIMA defines management accounting as:

'The application of the principles of accounting and financial management to create, protect, preserve and increase value for the _____ of for-profit and not-for profit enterprises in the public and private sectors.'
CIMA Official Terminology p18

    ○   Auditors
    ○   Stakeholders
    ○   Owners
    ○   Customers

6   Which of the following statements are true?

1   The main role of the management accountant is to produce financial accounts.
2   Management accountants always work within the finance function.
3   Management accountants always work in partnership with business manager.

    ○   1 and 2 only
    ○   2 and 3 only
    ○   1 and 3 only
    ○   None of the above

7 Which of the following statements about CIMA are true?

Select all that apply.

- ☐ CIMA was established over 90 years ago.
- ☐ CIMA members may only work in the UK.
- ☐ CIMA members and students must comply with the CIMA code of ethics.
- ☐ CIMA members work mainly on the production of financial accounts.
- ☐ CIMA members are not qualified to work as finance directors.
- ☐ CIMA members work in all areas of business.

8 Which of the below roles is NOT performed by a management accountant?

- ○ Planning short run operations
- ○ Providing information for the preparation of statutory financial statements
- ○ Controlling operations
- ○ Implementing corporate governance

9 Monthly variance reports are an example of which of the following types of management information?

- ○ Managerial
- ○ Strategic
- ○ Non-financial
- ○ Operational

10 Which of the following statements is correct?

- ○ Management accounting systems provide information for use in fulfilling legal requirements.
- ○ Management accounting systems provide information for the use of decision makers within an organisation.
- ○ Management accounting systems provide information for use by shareholders.
- ○ Management accounting systems provide information for use by tax authorities.

11 Who is responsible for planning, control and decision making in a business?

- ○ Shareholders or owners
- ○ Management
- ○ Supervisors
- ○ Auditors

12 Which of the following is NOT a quality of good information?

- ○ Accuracy
- ○ Completeness
- ○ Complexity
- ○ Relevance

The following information relates to questions 13, 14 and 15

These questions are on the Global Management Accounting Principles.

13   Which FOUR of the following are the Global Management Accounting Principles?

- [ ] Sustainable organisations achieve long term economic performance
- [ ] Stewardship builds trust
- [ ] Communication provides insight that is influential
- [ ] The letter and the spirit of laws, codes and regulations are followed
- [ ] Impact on value is analysed
- [ ] Information is relevant

14   Which FOUR of the following are the objectives associated with the Global Management Accounting Principles?

- [ ] To help organisations plan for and source the information needed for creating strategy and tactics for execution
- [ ] To actively manage relationships and resources so that the financial and non-financial assets, reputation and value of the organisation are protected
- [ ] To ensure that management accounting professionals are answerable to their direct customers about the decisions they make
- [ ] To help avoid conflicts of interest and making short-term decisions to the detriment of long-term success
- [ ] To simulate different scenarios that demonstrate the cause-and-effect relationships between inputs and outcomes
- [ ] To drive better decisions about strategy and its execution

15   Are the following statements true or false?

	True	False
The Global Management Accounting Principles were created to support organisations in benchmarking and improving their management accounting systems.	[ ]	[ ]
The foundation of the Global Management Accounting Principles is that an effective management accounting function improves decision making.	[ ]	[ ]

16 Management accounting and financial accounting analyse data and information in different ways.

For each of the following features, select whether it relates to management accounting or financial accounting.

	Management accounting	Financial accounting
Information focuses on the needs of internal management	☐	☐
Information can be presented in any format	☐	☐
Information relates to both the future and the past	☐	☐
Information is specified by law	☐	☐

17 Which of the following is a disadvantage of business process outsourcing?

- ○ Increased confidentiality of financial information
- ○ Reduced access to specialist knowledge
- ○ Less control over the finance function
- ○ Duplication of effort

18 Which TWO of the following tasks are carried out by management accountants?

- ☐ Preparation of cash budgets
- ☐ Helping with planning within the organisation
- ☐ Checking the accuracy of year end financial statements
- ☐ Preparation of the statement of profit or loss

19 Which of the following statements is true?

- ○ Strategic tasks are highly structured
- ○ Operational tasks are short term in timescale
- ○ Tactical information is mostly external
- ○ Operational plans are implemented by top level management

20 Seb works as a supervisor in department B of T Co. He is looking at short-term, detailed information about expenses in department B. Jai is looking at long-term loan options from various banks for T Co.

Which levels of information are Seb and Jai working with?

- ○ Seb: Strategic information Jai: Management information
- ○ Seb: Operational information Jai: Strategic information
- ○ Seb: Strategic information Jai: Operational information
- ○ Seb: Management information Jai: Strategic information

2 Costing

1   Which of the following items might be a suitable cost unit within the accounts payable department of a company?

    1   Postage cost
    2   Invoice processed
    3   Supplier account

    O   Item 1 only
    O   Item 2 only
    O   Item 3 only
    O   Items 2 and 3 only

2   Which of the following costs are part of the prime cost for a manufacturing company?

    O   Cost of transporting raw materials from the supplier's premises
    O   Wages of factory workers engaged in machine maintenance
    O   Depreciation of lorries used for deliveries to customers
    O   Cost of indirect production materials

3   Which of the following are true of depreciation on production equipment?

Select all that apply.

    ☐   It is not a cash cost
    ☐   It is part of production overheads
    ☐   It is part of prime cost
    ☐   It is always calculated using a machine-hour rate

4   A company makes chairs and tables.

Which THREE of the following items are treated as direct costs?

    ☐   Wood used to make a chair
    ☐   Metal used for the legs of a chair
    ☐   Fabric to cover the seat of a chair
    ☐   The salary of the sales director of the company
    ☐   Depreciation of delivery vehicles

5   The audit fee paid by a manufacturing company are classified by that company as:

    O   A production overhead cost
    O   A selling and distribution cost
    O   A research and development cost
    O   An administration cost

6   Cost centres are:

- ○   Units of output or service for which costs are ascertained
- ○   Functions or locations for which costs are ascertained
- ○   A segment of the organisation for which budgets are prepared
- ○   Amounts of expenditure attributable to various activities

7   Which of the following costs would NOT be classified as a production overhead cost in a food processing company?

- ○   The cost of renting the factory building
- ○   The salary of the factory manager
- ○   The depreciation of equipment located in the materials store
- ○   The cost of ingredients

8   A production manager's salary in a factory that makes one product can be classified as:

- ○   Direct expense
- ○   Direct labour
- ○   Indirect expense
- ○   Indirect labour

9   Which of the following is an example of direct labour for a company manufacturing cars?

- ○   Cook
- ○   Stores assistant
- ○   Factory accountant
- ○   Assembly line worker

10   Which of the following best describes a controllable cost?

- ○   A cost that arises from a decision already taken, which cannot, in the short run, be changed.
- ○   A cost for which the behaviour pattern can be easily analysed, in order to facilitate valid budgetary control comparisons.
- ○   A cost that can be influenced by its budget holder.
- ○   A specific cost of an activity or business that would be avoided if the activity or business did not exist.

11   For decision-making purposes, which THREE of the following are relevant costs?

- ☐   Avoidable cost
- ☐   Future cost
- ☐   Sunk cost
- ☐   Differential cost
- ☐   Committed cost

12   L Co is a badminton racquet manufacturer.

Select the correct entries below to match the correct cost type to each cost item.

Selling and distribution costs
Direct materials
Indirect labour
Direct labour
Administration costs

Cost item	Cost type
Carbon for racquet heads	
Office stationery	
Wages of employees stringing racquets	
Supervisors' salaries	
Advertising stand at badminton tournaments	

The following information relates to questions 13, 14 and 15

ZK has been asked to quote a price for a special job that must be completed within one week.

General fixed overheads are estimated at 10% of total production cost.

The job requires a total of 100 skilled labour hours and 50 unskilled labour hours. The current employees are paid a guaranteed minimum wage of $525 for skilled workers and $280 for unskilled workers for a 35-hour week.

Currently, skilled labour has spare capacity amounting to 75 labour hours each week and unskilled labour has spare capacity amounting to 100 labour hours each week.

Additional skilled workers and unskilled workers can be employed and paid by the hour at rates based on the wages paid to the current workers. The materials required for the job are currently held in inventory at a book value of $5,000. The materials are regularly used by ZK and the current replacement cost for the materials is $4,500. The total scrap value of the materials is $1,000.

13   What is the relevant cost to ZK of using the materials in inventory on this job?

   ○ $1,000
   ○ $3,500
   ○ $4,500
   ○ $5,000

14   What is the total relevant cost to ZK of using skilled and unskilled labour on this job?

   ○   Nil
   ○ $375
   ○ $775
   ○ $1,540

BPP
LEARNING
MEDIA

15   Which statement correctly describes the treatment of the general fixed overheads when preparing a quote on a relevant cost basis?

   O   The overheads should be excluded because they are a sunk cost.
   O   The overheads should be excluded because they are not incremental costs.
   O   The overheads should be included because they relate to production costs.
   O   The overheads should be included because all fixed costs should be recovered.

3 Cost behaviour

1   Variable costs are conventionally deemed to:

   O   Be constant per unit of output
   O   Vary per unit of output as production volume changes
   O   Be constant in total when production volume changes
   O   Vary, in total, from period to period when production is constant

2   The following is a graph of cost against level of activity:

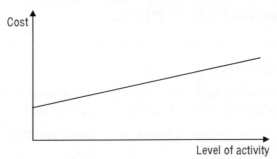

   To which of the following costs does the graph correspond?

   O   Electricity bills made up of a standing charge and a variable charge
   O   Bonus payment to employees when production reaches a certain level
   O   Salesperson's commissions payable per unit up to a maximum amount of commission
   O   Bulk discounts on purchases – the discount being given on all units purchased

3   B Co has recorded the following data in the two most recent periods.

Total cost of production	Volume of production
$	Units
13,500	700
18,300	1,100

   What is the best estimate of the company's fixed costs per period?

   O $13,500
   O $13,200
   O $5,100
   O $4,800

4   A hotel has recorded that the laundry costs incurred were $570 when 340 guests stayed for one night. They know that the fixed laundry cost is $400 per night.

What is the variable laundry cost per guest night (to the nearest cent)?

$ [   ]

5   The diagram below represents the behaviour of a cost item as the level of output changes.

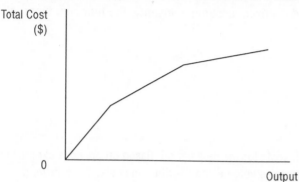

Which of the following situations is described by the graph?

○   Discounts are received on additional purchases of material when certain quantities are purchased.

○   Employees are paid a guaranteed weekly wage, together with bonuses for higher levels of production.

○   A licence is purchased from the government which allows unlimited production.

○   Additional space is rented to cope with the need to increase production.

6   A hospital's records show that the cost of carrying out health checks in the last five accounting periods has been as follows:

Period	Number of patients seen	Total cost $
1	650	17,125
2	940	17,800
3	1260	18,650
4	990	17,980
5	1150	18,360

Using the high-low method and ignoring inflation, the estimated cost of carrying out health checks on 850 patients in period 6 is:

○ $17,515
○ $17,570
○ $17,625
○ $17,680

7   The following data have been collected for four cost types; W, X, Y, and Z at two activity levels.

Cost type	Cost @ 100 units	Cost @ 140 units
W	8,000	10,560
X	5,000	5,000
Y	6,500	9,100
Z	6,700	8,580

Where V = variable, SV = semi-variable and F = fixed, assuming linearity, the four cost types W, X, Y and Z are respectively:

	W	X	Y	Z
○	V	F	SV	V
○	SV	F	V	SV
○	V	F	V	V
○	SV	F	SV	SV

8   DP Co is preparing its estimate of distribution costs for the next period. Based on previous experience, a linear relationship has been identified between sales volume and distribution costs. The following information has been collected concerning distribution costs.

Sales volume	Distribution cost
Units	$
22,000	58,600
34,000	73,000

What would be the estimated distribution costs for a sales volume of 28,000 units?

○ $32,200
○ $33,600
○ $65,800
○ $74,582

9   A company's weekly costs ($C) were plotted against production level (P) for the last 50 weeks and a regression line calculated to be C = 200 + 30P.

What are the values of the variable costs per unit?

10   HF Co has noticed that there is a correlation between the number of units produced (x) and the cost (y). There is a fixed element to the cost (called a) and a variable element (called b). The accounts assistant has started regression analysis.

If $\Sigma x = 60$, $\Sigma y = 1048$, $\Sigma xy = 7092$, $\Sigma x^2 = 440$ and n = 10, what is the value of a in the equation y = a + bx if b = 10.05?

(to 1 decimal place)

11   CF Co has noticed that there is a correlation between the number of units produced (x) and the cost (y). There is a fixed element to the cost (called a) and a variable element (called b). The accounts assistant has started regression analysis.

If $\Sigma x = 9$, $\Sigma y = 45$, $\Sigma xy = 83$, $\Sigma x^2 = 19$ and $n = 5$, what is the value of b in the equation $y = a + bx$?

(to 2 decimal places)

```

```

12   Observed costs at different production levels were as follows.

Output units	Total costs
	$
160	32,000
240	44,500
350	49,100

What is the value of the fixed costs?

(to the nearest $)

$ [   ]

The following information relates to questions 13, 14 and 15

Level of activity
Graph 1

Level of activity
Graph 2

Level of activity
Graph 3

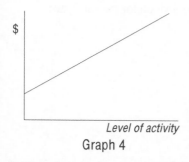

Level of activity
Graph 4

Level of activity
Graph 5

Level of activity
Graph 6

Which of the above graphs illustrates the costs described in the next three questions?

BPP
LEARNING
MEDIA

13   A linear variable cost – when the vertical axis represents cost incurred

    ○   Graph 1
    ○   Graph 2
    ○   Graph 4
    ○   Graph 5

14   A linear variable cost – when the vertical axis represents cost per unit

    ○   Graph 1
    ○   Graph 2
    ○   Graph 3
    ○   Graph 6

15   A stepped fixed cost – when the vertical axis represents cost incurred

    ○   Graph 3
    ○   Graph 4
    ○   Graph 5
    ○   Graph 6

16   East Co suspects that there is a relationship between the number of units sold and the number of units returned as faulty. x = number of units sold and y = number of returns.

If $\sum x = 440$, $\sum y = 330$, $\sum x^2 = 17,986$, $\sum y^2 = 10,366$, $\sum xy = 13,467$ and n = 11, then the value of r, the coefficient of correlation, to 2 decimal places, is [　　　　　]

17   The value of the correlation coefficient between x (output) and y (production costs) is 0.9. Which of the following is correct?

    ○   There is a weak relationship between x and y.
    ○   x is 90% of y.
    ○   If the values of x and y were plotted on a graph, the line relating them would have a slope of 0.9.
    ○   There is a very strong relationship between x and y.

18   If the correlation coefficient for two variables is –0.8, the coefficient of determination for the same two variables is [　　　　　] (Give your answer to 2 decimal places)

4 Absorption costing

1   The process of cost apportionment is carried out so that:

    ○   Costs may be controlled
    ○   Cost units gather overheads as they pass through cost centres
    ○   Whole items of cost can be charged to cost centres
    ○   Common costs are shared among cost centres

2   The following extract of information is available concerning the four cost centres of EG Co.

	Production cost centres			Service cost centre
	Machinery	Finishing	Packing	Canteen
Number of direct employees	7	6	2	–
Number of indirect employees	3	2	1	4
Overhead allocated and apportioned	$28,500	$18,300	$8,960	$8,400

The overhead cost of the canteen is to be re-apportioned to the production cost centres on the basis of the number of employees in each production cost centre.

After the re-apportionment, the total overhead cost of the packing department (to the nearest $) will be:

  ○ $1,200
  ○ $9,968
  ○ $10,080
  ○ $10,160

---

3   A company absorbs overheads on machine hours that were budgeted at 11,250 with overheads of $258,750. The actual results were 10,980 hours with overheads of $254,692.

Overheads were:

  ○   Under absorbed by $2,152
  ○   Over absorbed by $4,058
  ○   Under absorbed by $4,058
  ○   Over absorbed by $2,152

---

4   A company absorbs overheads on the basis of machine hours.

In a period, actual machine hours were 22,435, actual overheads were $496,500 and there was over absorption of $64,375.

What was the budgeted overhead absorption rate per machine hour (to the nearest $)?

$ [＿＿＿＿＿＿＿＿]

---

5   A company uses the repeated distribution method to reapportion service department costs. The use of this method suggests:

  ○   The company's overhead rates are based on estimates of cost and activity levels, rather than actual amounts.

  ○   There are more service departments than production cost centres.

  ○   The company wishes to avoid under or over absorption of overheads in its production cost.

  ○   The service departments carry out work for each other.

6   Based on the data below, what is the amount of the overhead under-/over-absorbed?

Budgeted overheads	$493,200
Budgeted machine hours	10,960
Actual machine hours	10,493
Actual overheads	$514,157

- ○ $20,957 under absorbed
- ○ $21,015 over absorbed
- ○ $21,015 under absorbed
- ○ $41,972 under absorbed

---

7   Factory overheads can be absorbed by which of the following methods?

1   Direct labour hours
2   Machine hours
3   As a % of prime
4    $x per unit

- ○ 1, 2, 3 or 4
- ○ 1 and 2 only
- ○ 1, 2 or 3 only
- ○ 2, 3 or 4 only

---

8   Department L production overheads are absorbed using a direct labour hour rate. Budgeted production overheads for the department were $480,000, and the actual labour hours were 100,000. Actual production overheads amounted to $516,000.

Based on the above data, and assuming that the production overheads were over absorbed by $24,000, what was the overhead absorption rate per labour hour?

- ○ $4.80
- ○ $4.92
- ○ $5.16
- ○ $5.40

---

9   MEB Co has two production cost centres (H and J) and two service cost centres (stores and canteen). Service cost centres do work for each other and the production departments in the following proportions.

Stores	$160,000	*Canteen*	$80,000
Production centre H	35%	Production centre H	50%
Production centre J	35%	Production centre J	45%
Canteen	30%	Stores	5%

After repeated distribution, how much of the service department costs will end up in Production centre J (to the nearest hundred $)?

$ [   ]

10   Are the following statements about predetermined overhead absorption rates true or false?

                                                                                                      True False

    1   Using a predetermined absorption rate avoids fluctuations in unit costs caused by
           abnormally high or low overhead expenditure or activity levels.   ☐   ☐

    2   Using a predetermined absorption rate offers the administrative convenience of
           being able to record full production costs sooner.   ☐   ☐

    3   Using a predetermined absorption rate avoids problems of under/over absorption
           of overheads because a constant overhead rate is available.   ☐   ☐

11   ABC Co absorbs fixed production overheads in one of its departments on the basis of machine hours. There
      were 100,000 budgeted machine hours for the forthcoming period. The fixed production overhead
      absorption rate was $2.50 per machine hour.

      During the period, the following actual results were recorded:

      Machine hours 110,000

      Fixed production overheads $300,000

      Which of the following statements is correct?

      ○   Overhead was $25,000 over-absorbed
      ○   Overhead was $25,000 under-absorbed
      ○   Overhead was $50,000 over-absorbed
      ○   No under or over absorption occurred

12   Which of the following would be the most appropriate basis for apportioning machinery insurance costs to
      cost centres within a factory?

      ○   The number of machines in each cost centre
      ○   The floor area occupied by the machinery in each cost centre
      ○   The value of the machinery in each cost centre
      ○   The operating hours of the machinery in each cost centre

The following information relates to questions 13, 14 and 15

Budgeted information relating to two departments in JP Co for quarter 1 is as follows.

Department	Production overhead $	Direct material cost $	Direct labour cost $	Direct labour hours	Machine hours
1	27,000	67,500	13,500	2,700	45,000
2	18,000	36,000	100,000	25,000	300

Individual direct labour employees within each department earn differing rates of pay, according to their skills, grade and experience.

13   What is the most appropriate production overhead absorption rate for department 1?

○   40% of direct material cost
○   200% of direct labour cost
○ $10 per direct labour hour
○ $0.60 per machine hour

14   What is the most appropriate production overhead absorption rate for department 2?

○   50% of direct material cost
○   18% of direct labour cost
○ $0.72 per direct labour hour
○ $60 per machine hour

15   In quarter 2, department 2 decided to use an absorption rate based on the number of units. Department 2 over absorbed fixed production overheads for quarter 2 by $6,000. The fixed production overhead absorption rate was $8 per unit and is based on the normal level of activity of 5,000 units. Actual production was 4,500 units.

What was the actual fixed production overheads incurred for the period?

○ $30,000
○ $36,000
○ $40,000
○ $42,000

16   Paris Co's budgeted overheads for next year include:

Depreciation of plant and equipment $2,010,000
Power for production machinery $1,787,500
Rent and rates $261,000

Overheads are apportioned on the most appropriate basis to the silicon moulding production cost centre and the silicon extrusion production cost centre.

The following information is also available:

	Net book value of equipment	Machinery power usage (KwH)	Floor space sq metres	No. of employees
	$'000	'000		
Silicon moulding	3,600	1,145	8,000	15
Silicon extrusion	4,400	2,430	12,000	16
Total	8,000	3,575	20,000	31

What value of overheads will be apportioned to the silicon moulding production cost centre? Work to nearest $.

$ _____

BPP
LEARNING
MEDIA

5 Marginal costing and pricing decisions

1   When opening inventories were 8,500 litres and closing inventories were 6,750 litres, a firm had a profit of $27,400 using marginal costing. Assuming that the fixed overhead absorption rate was $2 per litre, the profit using absorption costing would be $ [   ] .

2   Duo Co makes and sells two products, Alpha and Beta. The following information is available for period 1.

	Production Units	Sales Units
Alpha	2,500	2,300
Beta	1,750	1,600

	Product Alpha $	Beta $
Unit selling price	90	75
Unit variable costs		
Direct materials	15	12
Direct labour ($6/hr)	18	12
Variable production overheads	12	8

Fixed costs for the company in total were $110,000 in period 1 and are recovered on the basis of direct labour hours.

The profit reported for period 1 using marginal costing principles is $ [   ] .

3   Product X is produced in two production cost centres. Budgeted data for product X are as follows.

	Cost centre A	Cost centre B
Direct material cost per unit	$60.00	$30.30
Direct labour hours per unit	3	1
Direct labour rate per hour	$20.00	$15.20
Production overhead absorption rate per direct labour hour	$12.24	$14.94

General overhead costs are absorbed into product costs at a rate of 10% of production cost.

If a 20% return on sales is required from product X, its selling price per unit should be, to the nearest $0.01:

- ○ $260.59
- ○ $271.45
- ○ $286.66
- ○ $298.60

4   Cost and selling price details for product Q are as follows.

	$ per unit
Direct material	4.20
Direct labour	3.00
Variable overhead	1.00
Fixed overhead	2.80
	11.00
Profit	4.00
Selling price	15.00

Budgeted production for month	10,000 units
Actual production for month	12,000 units
Actual sales for month	11,200 units
Actual fixed overhead cost incurred during month	$31,000

Based on the above data, the marginal costing profit for the month is:

- ○ $44,800
- ○ $45,160
- ○ $50,600
- ○ $76,160

5   The overhead absorption rate for product T is $4 per machine hour. Each unit of T requires 3 machine hours. Inventories of product T last period were:

	Units
Opening inventory	2,400
Closing inventory	2,700

Compared with the marginal costing profit for the period, the absorption costing profit for product T will be which of the following?

- ○ $1,200 higher
- ○ $3,600 higher
- ○ $1,200 lower
- ○ $3,600 lower

6   Last month a manufacturing company's profit was $2,000, calculated using absorption costing principles. If marginal costing principles has been used, a loss of $3,000 would have occurred. The company's fixed production cost is $2 per unit. Sales last month were 10,000 units.

What was last month's production (in units)?

- ○ 7,500
- ○ 9,500
- ○ 10,500
- ○ 12,500

7   A company budgets to make 50,000 units that have a variable cost of production of $10 per unit. Fixed production costs are $150,000 per annum. If the selling price is to be 35% higher than full cost, what is the selling price of the product using the full cost-plus method?

$ [   ]

8   A technical writer is to set up her own business. She anticipates working a 40-hour week and taking four weeks' holiday per year. General expenses of the business are expected to be $10,000 per year, and she has set herself a target of $40,000 a year salary.

Assuming that only 90% of her time worked will be chargeable to customers, her charge for each hour of writing (to the nearest cent) should be:

$ [   ]

9   A company produces and sells a single product whose variable cost is $15 per unit. Fixed costs have been absorbed over the normal level of activity of 500,000 units and have been calculated as $5 per unit. The current selling price is $25 per unit.

How much profit is made under marginal costing if the company sells 625,000 units?

$ [   ]

10   The overhead absorption rate for product M is $6 per unit. Inventories of product M in the last period were:

	Units
Opening inventory	2,500
Closing inventory	2,100

Compared with the marginal costing profit for the period, the absorption costing profit for product M will be:

O $400 higher
O $2,400 higher
O $400 lower
O $2,400 lower

11   Last month, when a company had an opening inventory of 16,500 units and a closing inventory of 18,000 units, the profit using absorption costing was $40,000. The fixed production overhead rate was $10 per unit.

What would the profit for last month have been using marginal costing?

O $15,000
O $25,000
O $55,000
O $65,000

12   The following data relate to the Super.

Material cost per unit	$15.00
Labour cost per unit	$52.05
Production overhead cost per machine hour	$9.44
Machine hours per unit	7
General overhead absorption rate	8% of total production cost

The capital invested in manufacturing and distributing 9,530 units of the Super per annum is estimated to be $3,620,000.

If the required annual rate of return on capital invested in each product is 14%, the selling price per unit of the Super is, to the nearest $0.01:

$ [   ]

The following information relates to questions 13, 14 and 15

Given below is the standard cost of a product:

	$
Direct material	6.00
Direct labour	7.50
Variable overhead	2.50
Fixed overhead absorption rate	5.00
	21.00
Profit	9.00
Selling price	30.00

Budgeted production for the month of June was 5,000 units although the company managed to produce 5,800 units, selling 5,200 of them and incurring fixed overhead costs of $27,400. At the end of July, there were 800 units of closing inventory. Opening inventory at 1 June was nil.

13   What was the marginal costing profit for the month?

○ $45,400
○ $46,800
○ $53,800
○ $72,800

14   What was the absorption costing profit for the month?

○ $45,200
○ $45,400
○ $56,800
○ $48,400

15 How did the profits compare in July under marginal costing and absorption costing?

○ Profit under absorption costing was higher than under marginal costing by $1,000.
○ Profit under marginal costing was higher than under absorption costing by $1,000.
○ Profit under absorption costing was higher than under marginal costing by $4,000.
○ Profit under marginal costing was higher than under absorption costing by $4,000.

16 Yumm Co uses marginal cost plus pricing and has recently developed a new type of cake which will be sold in batches. The costs per batch are as follows:

Variable ingredients	3 kg @ $1.20 per kg
Variable labour	2 hours @ $15 per hour
Variable overheads	1 hour @ $7 per hour
Absorbed fixed overheads	2 hours @ $12 per hour

What is the selling price per batch if Yumm Co wants to achieve a margin of 30% (to the nearest whole number)?

$ [   ]

6 Breakeven analysis

1 A Co makes a single product which it sells for $10 per unit. Fixed costs are $48,000 per month and the product has a contribution to sales ratio of 40%. In a month when actual sales were $140,000, A Co's margin of safety, in units, was:

○ 2,000
○ 12,000
○ 14,000
○ 20,000

2

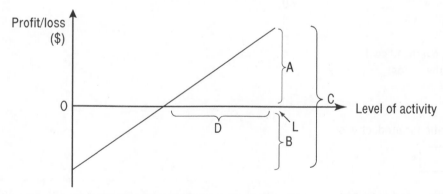

In the above profit-volume chart, the contribution at level of activity L can be read as:

○ Distance A
○ Distance B
○ Distance C
○ Distance D

BPP
LEARNING
MEDIA

3   Data concerning K CO's single product is as follows.

	$ per unit
Selling price	6.00
Variable production cost	1.20
Variable selling cost	0.40
Fixed production cost	4.00
Fixed selling cost	0.80

Budgeted production and sales for the year are 10,000 units.

It is now expected that the variable production cost per unit and the selling price per unit will each increase by 10%, and fixed production costs will rise by 25%.

What will the new breakeven point be, to the nearest whole unit?

○   8,788 units
○   11,600 units
○   11,886 units
○   12,397 units

4   Crasher Co budgets to make and sell 4,000 units of product. The selling price of the product is $7. This price was calculated using the following unit cost information.

Variable cost	$2.60
Fixed cost	$1.10
Total	$3.70

Calculate the margin of safety ratio of Crasher Co's sales (as a percentage of budgeted sales). The margin of safety ratio is [   ] % of budget.

5   S Co manufactures a single product, V. Data for the product are as follows.

	$ per unit
Selling price	40
Direct material cost	8
Direct labour cost	6
Variable production overhead cost	4
Variable selling overhead cost	2
Fixed overhead cost	10
Profit per unit	10

The profit/volume ratio for product V is:

[   ] %

6   F Scuttle Co has fixed costs of $50,000 per annum. The company sells a single product for $25 per unit. The contribution to sales ratio is 40%.

What is the breakeven point in revenue?

$ [   ]

BPP
LEARNING
MEDIA

7   Product N generates a contribution to sales ratio of 20%. Annual fixed costs are $80,000. The selling price per unit is $50. The breakeven point, in terms of units sold per annum, is:

○   96,000
○   400,000
○   480,000
○   8,000

8   Which THREE of the following statements concerning cost-volume-profit (CVP) analysis are true?

☐   Changes in inventory levels are ignored.
☐   Only one product at a time can be analysed on a breakeven chart.
☐   A change in the estimate of fixed costs will alter the slope of the line on a profit-volume (PV) chart.
☐   A change in the selling price per unit will alter the slope of the line on a P/V chart.
☐   An assumption is made that variable costs per unit are the same at all levels of output.

9   Marker Co makes a single product, the Whizzo. This product sells for $10, and makes a contribution of $5 per unit. Total fixed costs per annum are $12,518.

If Maker Co wishes to make an annual profit of $8,982, how many Whizzos do they need to sell?

    | | units

10   A single product company has a contribution to sales ratio of 40%. Fixed costs amount to $90,000 per annum. The selling price per unit is $25.

The number of units required to break even is:

○   9,000
○   36,000
○   150,000
○   225,000

11   B Co manufactures and sells a single product, with the following estimated costs for next year.

	Unit cost	
	100,000 units of output	*150,000 units of output*
	$	$
Direct materials	20.00	20.00
Direct labour	5.00	5.00
Production overheads	10.00	7.50
Marketing costs	7.50	5.00
Administration costs	5.00	4.00
	47.50	41.50

Fixed costs are unaffected by the volume of output.

B Co's management think they can sell 150,000 units per annum if the sales price is $49.50.

The breakeven point, in units, at this price is:

○   36,364
○   90,000
○   101,020
○   225,000

12

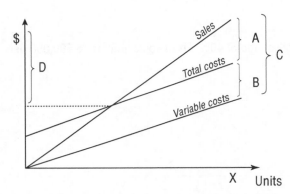

In the above breakeven chart, the contribution at level of activity x can be read as:

○   Distance A
○   Distance B
○   Distance C
○   Distance D

The following information relates to questions 13, 14 and 15

Fast Fandango Co manufactures a single product, the FF, which sells for $10. At 75% capacity, which is the normal level of activity for the factory, sales are $600,000 per period.

The cost of these sales are as follows.

Direct cost per unit	$3
Production overhead	$156,000 (including variable costs of $30,000)
Sales costs	$80,000
Distribution costs	$60,000 (including variable costs of $15,000)
Administration overhead	$40,000 (including variable costs of $9,000)

The sales costs are fixed with the exception of sales commission, which is 5% of sales value.

---

13   The contribution per unit of product FF is:

$ [   ]

---

14   The fixed cost per period is:

$ [   ]

---

15   The breakeven volume of sales per period is [   ] units.

---

16   Lime Co makes a single product and incurs fixed production costs of $90,000 per month and fixed selling costs of $240,000 per year. Budgeted sales revenue for June is $200,000 and budgeted contribution for June is $80,000.

What is the breakeven sales revenue for June?

$ [   ]

---

7 Limiting factor analysis

1   A company manufactures three products, details of which are as follows.

	Product J $ per unit	Product K $ per unit	Product L $ per unit
Selling price	140	122	134
Direct materials ($2/kg)	22	14	26
Other variable cost	84	72	51
Fixed cost	20	26	40

In a period when direct material is restricted in supply, the ranking of the products in terms of the most profitable use of the material is:

First product   [　　　　　　　]

Second product   [　　　　　　　]

Third product   [　　　　　　　]

---

2   SIM Co manufactures three products, the selling price and cost details of which are given below.

	Product A	Product B	Product C
	$	$	$
Selling price per unit	375	475	475
Costs per unit			
Direct materials ($5/kg)	50	25	75
Direct labour ($4/hour)	80	120	100
Variable overhead	40	60	50
Fixed overhead	120	180	150

In a period when direct materials are restricted in supply, the most and least profitable uses of direct materials are:

	Most profitable	Least profitable
O	B	C
O	C	A
O	B	A
O	C	B

---

3   A company makes a single product for which standard cost details are as follows.

	$ per unit
Direct material ($8 per litre)	72
Direct labour ($7 per hour)	49
Production overhead	56
Total production cost	177

The product is perishable and no inventories are held.

Demand for next period will be 2,000 units but only 16,000 litres of material and 15,000 hours of labour will be available. The limiting factor(s) next period will be:

O   Material only
O   Labour only
O   Material and labour
O   Neither material nor labour

4   TTT Co makes three products. All three use the same machine, which is available for 125,000 hours per period.

The standard costs of the products per unit are as follows.

	Product T1 $	Product T2 $	Product T3 $
Direct labour:			
Machinists ($11 per hour)	55	33	66
Maximum demand (units)	9,000	8,000	11,000

The deficiency in machine hours for the next period is ⬚ hours.

---

5   FEEB manufactures two products, the FE and the EB, using the same material for each.

Annual demand for the FE is 10,000 units, while demand for the EB is 7,000 units.

The variable production cost per unit of the FE is $15, while that of the EB is $21. The FE requires 1.5 kg of raw material per unit, and the EB requires 2 kg of raw material per unit. Supply of raw material will be limited to 25,000 kg during the year.

A subcontractor has quoted prices of $24 per unit for the FE and $27 per unit for the EB to supply the product. How many units of each product should FEEB manufacture in order to maximise profits?

FE: ⬚ units

EB: ⬚ units

---

6   J Co manufactures three products, details of which are as follows.

	Product K $ per unit	Product L $ per unit	Product M $ per unit
Selling price	105	133	133
Direct materials ($3/litre)	15	6	21
Direct labour ($8/hour)	24	32	24
Variable overhead	9	12	9
Fixed overhead	23	50	42

In a period when direct labour is restricted in supply, the most and least profitable use of labour are:

	Most profitable	Least profitable
○	K	M
○	L	K
○	M	K
○	M	L

7   A company makes three products, to which the following budget information relates.

	B	A	T
Selling price	100	120	145
Labour at $20 per hour	40	40	60
Materials at $10 per kg	10	20	30
Fixed overheads	30	40	20
Profit	20	20	35

The marketing department says that maximum annual sales are 1,000 units of product B, 1,200 units of product A and 1,500 units of product T. The factory has budgeted to make that number of units. It has just been discovered that next year materials will be limited to 5,000 kg and labour to 10,000 hours.

If the company wishes to maximise profit, the priority in which the products should be made and sold is:

○   B A T
○   A B T
○   T A B
○   T B A

---

8   A company makes three products and has produced the following standard cost cards.

	X $ per unit	Y $ per unit	Z $ per unit
Selling price	100	80	70
Variable costs			
Material	20	30	5
Labour	30	10	5
Fixed overheads	40	10	40
Profit	10	30	20

The same labour is used to make all three products, but in different quantities.

In a month when expenditure on labour is restricted to $50,000, what is the maximum contribution that can be earned?

Assume that the company can make and sell any combination of products.

$ [   ]

---

9   When using limiting factor analysis in order to calculate maximum profit, which THREE of the following assumptions should be made?

☐   Fixed costs per unit are not changed by changes in production.

☐   Fixed costs in total are not changed by changes in production.

☐   Variable costs per unit are not changed by changes in production.

☐   Variable costs in total are not changed by changes in production.

☐   Sales demand, prices and resources required for each product are known with certainty.

10 A company makes three products, to which the following budgeted information relates.

	B	A	T
Selling price	100	120	145
Labour at $20 per hour	40	40	60
Materials at $10 per kg	10	20	30
Fixed overheads	30	40	20
Profit	20	20	35

The marketing department says that maximum annual sales are: 1,000 units of product B, 1,200 units of Product A and 1,500 units of Product T. Budgeted production levels for the year are the same as maximum annual sales.

It has just been discovered that materials will be limited to 5,000 kg per year. The company does not hold any finished inventory. The products have been correctly ranked by contribution per kg as follows:

	B	A	T
Contribution per unit ($)	50	60	55
Kg of material per unit	1	2	3
Contribution per kg of material ($)	50	30	18.3
Rank by contribution per kg of material	1	2	3

Calculate the maximum profit for next year.

$ [   ]

---

11 A company manufactures three products, X, Y and Z.

	Product X $ per unit	Product Y $ per unit	Product Z $ per unit
Variable cost	5.00	16.00	10.00
Fixed cost	4.00	16.60	7.50
Total unit cost	9.00	32.60	17.50

The fixed costs are an allocation of general fixed overheads. A supplier has offered to supply the components at the following prices:

Component X $8
Component Y $14
Component Z $11

Which products should be purchased externally?

O   Components X and Z
O   Component Y only
O   None of the components
O   All of the components

12 V Co manufactures three products which have the following selling prices and costs per unit.

	V1 $	V2 $	V3 $
Selling price	30.00	36.00	34.00
Costs per unit			
Direct materials	8.00	10.00	20.00
Direct labour	4.00	8.00	3.60
Overhead			
Variable	2.00	4.00	1.80
Fixed	9.00	6.00	2.70
	23.00	28.00	28.10
Profit per unit	7.00	8.00	5.90

All three products use the same type of labour.

In a period in which labour is in short supply, the rank order of production is:

1st: V ☐

2nd: V ☐

3rd: V ☐

The following information relates to questions 13, 14 and 15

A company makes three products. All three use the same machine, which is available for 50,000 hours per period. The standard costs of the products per unit are as follows.

	Product A $	Product B $	Product C $
Direct materials	70	40	80
Direct labour:			
Machinists ($8 per hour)	48	32	56
Assemblers ($6 per hour)	36	40	42
Total variable cost	154	112	178
Selling price per unit	200	158	224
Maximum demand (units)	3,000	2,500	5,000

Fixed costs are $300,000 per period.

13 The deficiency in machine hours for the next period is ☐ hours.

14 In order to determine the priority ranking of the products, it is necessary to calculate the contribution per machine hour (as machine hours are the limiting factor). State your answers to 2 decimal places.

Contribution per machine hour (Product A) = $ ☐

Contribution per machine hour (Product B) = $ ☐

Contribution per machine hour (Product C) = $ ☐

15 If the optimum production plan includes manufacturing 2,500 units of product B, this product will generate a contribution of (to the nearest $):

$ [   ]

16 Jump Co currently makes and sells three products with costs per unit as follows:

	Spring	Ping	Ting
	$	$	$
Direct material	6	9	7
Direct labour	15	12	15
Allocated fixed overheads	10	12	12
Directly attributable fixed costs	5	2	3

Jump Co is considering whether it would be financially worthwhile to buy the products instead of making them and a supplier has offered to make the products for the following prices:

	Spring	Ping	Ting
Supplier price ($)	27	24	23

Which products should be purchased from the supplier?

- ○ Product Spring
- ○ Product Ping
- ○ Product Ting
- ○ None of the products

8 Standard costing

1 What is an attainable standard?

- ○ A standard that is based on currently attainable working conditions.

- ○ A standard that is established for use over a long period, and is used to show trends.

- ○ A standard that can be attained under perfect operating conditions, and which does not include an allowance for wastage, spoilage, machine breakdowns and other inefficiencies.

- ○ A standard that can be attained if production is carried out efficiently, machines are operated properly and/or materials are used properly. Some allowance is made for waste and inefficiencies.

2 Hopkins Co is expecting to make 2,500 units, with production being spread evenly over the year.

The budgeted production overhead is a fixed cost and amounts to $37,500. Absorption is based on units produced. The standard direct cost per unit is $23.

What is the standard total product cost?

$ [   ]

3   Bowdler Co makes and sells a simple product, the contemporary frying pan, with the following standard specification for materials.

	Quantity (Kg)	Price/Kg ($)
Raw material X	15	3
Raw material Y	8	4

It takes 2 direct labour hours to produce one frying pan. The standard direct labour cost is $6.25 per hour.

What is the standard direct cost of one frying pan?

$ [   ]

---

4   PM Co is in the process of setting standard unit costs for the next period. Period J uses two types of material: P and S. 7 kg of material P and 3 kg of material S are needed, at a standard price of $4 per kg and $9 per kg respectively.

Direct labour will cost $7 per hour and each unit of J requires 5 hours of labour.

Production overheads are to be recovered at the rate of $6 per direct labour hour, and general overhead is to be absorbed at a rate of 10% of production cost.

The standard prime cost for one unit of product J will be:

O $55
O $90
O $120
O $132

---

5   A toy manufacturer employs operatives to assemble toy aeroplanes. The operatives are paid a bonus of 25% of their basic hourly pay for any time saved by working more quickly than standard.

Basic hourly rate	$20
Bonus	25%
Standard hours	1.5

During June, the operatives assembled 1,200 aeroplanes in 1,500 hours.

Calculate the operatives' earnings for June.

$ [   ]

6   Wood Co manufactures garden sheds, garden tables and workbenches. In order to monitor trends in productivity they measure output in terms of standard hours. Actual results for the first week of October are shown below.

	Units produced	Standard time per unit Hours	Actual time taken Hours
Sheds	270	1.2	330
Tables	80	0.7	50
Workbenches	140	1.0	135

The number of standard hours produced was:

- O   490
- O   515
- O   520
- O   1,421

7   What is a standard hour?

- O   An operating hour in which there are no exceptional events, eg machine breakdowns
- O   An hour during which only standard units are made
- O   The amount of work achievable in an hour, when working at standard efficiency levels
- O   An hour during which only standard hourly rates are paid to labour

8   What is a basic standard?

- O   A standard that includes no allowance for losses, waste and inefficiencies. It represents the level of performance that is attainable under perfect operating conditions

- O   A standard that includes some allowance for losses, waste and inefficiencies. It represents the level of performance that is attainable under efficient operating conditions

- O   A standard that is based on currently attainable operating conditions

- O   A standard that is kept unchanged, to show the trend in costs

9   Which of the following statements is correct?

- O   The operating standards set for production should be the most ideal possible.
- O   The operating standards set for production should be the minimal level.
- O   The operating standards set for production should be the attainable level.
- O   The operating standards set for production should be the maximum level.

10   A company manufactures a carbonated drink, which is sold in 1 litre bottles. During the bottling process there is a 20% loss of liquid input due to spillage and evaporation. What is the standard usage of liquid per bottle?

- O   0.80 litres
- O   1.00 litres
- O   1.20 litres
- O   1.25 litres

11 Which of the following best describes management by exception?

○ Using management reports to highlight exceptionally good performance, so that favourable results can be built upon to improve future outcomes

○ Sending management reports only to those managers who are able to act on the information contained within the reports

○ Focusing management reports on areas that require attention and ignoring those that appear to be performing within acceptable limits

○ Focusing management reports on areas that are performing just outside of acceptable limits

12 Standard costing provides which of the following?

1 Targets and measures of performance
2 Information for budgeting
3 Simplification of inventory control systems
4 Actual future costs

○ 1, 2 and 3 only
○ 2, 3 and 4 only
○ 1, 3 and 4 only
○ 1, 2 and 4 only

The following information relates to questions 13, 14 and 15

FEB Co uses absorption costing. It has had problems with its machinery and there has been an increase in idle time. Staff are becoming demotivated and FEB Co has decided to recalculate its standards.

A unit of product L requires 9 active labour hours for completion. The standard for product L should allow for 10% of total labour time to be idle, due to the machine downtime. The standard wage rate is $9 per hour.

13 Which type of standard is most demotivating for staff?

○ Ideal
○ Attainable
○ Basic
○ Current

14 What is the standard labour cost per unit of product L?

○ $72.90
○ $81.00
○ $89.10
○ $90.00

15 Standard costs may only be used in an absorption costing system.

True ☐

False ☐

9 Flexible budgeting

1   Misty Co's budgetary control report for last month is as follows:

	Fixed budget $	Flexed budget $	Actual results $
Direct costs	61,100	64,155	67,130
Production overhead	55,000	56,700	54,950
Other overhead	10,000	10,000	11,500
	126,100	130,855	133,580

Favourable   Adverse

The volume variance for last month was $ [＿＿＿＿] [＿＿＿＿] [＿＿＿＿]

Tick either the adverse or favourable box as appropriate.

2   A flexible budget is:

○   A budget that, by recognising different cost behaviour patterns, is designed to change as the volume of activity changes

○   A budget for a defined period of time, which includes planned revenues, expenses, assets, liabilities and cash flow

○   A budget that is continuously updated as actual results are reported, adding further forecast periods

○   A budget of semi-variable production costs only

3
Budget	Actual
700 units	790 units
$29,400	$29,666

Which of the below options are relevant for comparison purposes?

	Budget	Actual
○	$29,400	$29,666
○	$29,400	$33,180
○	$33,180	$29,666
○	$700	$790

4   The following extract is taken from the overhead budget of X:

Budgeted activity	50%	75%
Budgeted overhead	$100,000	$112,500

The overhead budget for an activity level of 80% would be:

○ $115,000
○ $120,000
○ $136,000
○ $160,000

5   The following extract is taken from the production cost budget of H Co.

Production (units)   2,000   3,000
Production cost ($)   27,400   32,600

The budget cost allowance for an activity level of 4,000 units is:

$ [   ]

---

6   QT Co manufactures a single product and an extract from their flexed budget for production costs is as follows.

	Activity level	
	80%	90%
	$	$
Direct material	2,400	2,700
Direct labour	2,120	2,160
Production overhead	4,060	4,080
	8,580	8,940

The total production cost allowance in a budget flexed at the 83% level of activity would be, to the nearest $:

$ [   ]

---

7   Misty Co's budgetary control report for last month is as follows:

	Fixed budget	Flexed budget	Actual results
	$	$	$
Direct costs	61,100	64,155	67,130
Production overhead	55,000	56,700	54,950
Other overhead	10,000	10,000	11,500
	126,100	130,855	133,580

Favourable   Adverse

The expenditure variance for last month was $ [   ]   [   ]   [   ]

Tick either the adverse or favourable box as appropriate.

---

8   The following extract is taken from the production cost budget of S Co.

Production (units)   2,000   3,000
Production cost ($)   11,100   12,900

The budget cost allowance for an activity level of 4,000 units is:

O $7,200
O $7,500
O $13,460
O $14,700

9   The budgeted and actual figures for B Co are shown below for October. B Co uses a marginal costing system and all direct costs are wholly variable.

	Budget	Actual
Production/sales units	10,000	12,000
	$	$
Direct material	45,000	54,000
Direct labour	30,000	36,000
Variable overhead	20,000	24,000
Fixed overhead	25,000	25,000
Sales revenue	150,000	174,000

The profit shown by B Co's flexed budget for October would be:

O $11,000
O $30,000
O $36,000
O $41,000

---

10   A direct mail marketing company is setting the budgets for its next financial year.

In 20X2, costs were $1,077,000. In 20X3, activity was up 10% and costs were $1,100,000. Activity is expected to increase by 35% of the 20X3 levels in 20X4.

What is the expected total level of costs in 20X4?

$ ☐

---

11   CA Co manufactures a single product and has drawn up the following flexed budget for the year.

	60%	70%	80%
	$	$	$
Direct materials	120,000	140,000	160,000
Direct labour	90,000	105,000	120,000
Production overhead	54,000	58,000	62,000
Other overhead	40,000	40,000	40,000
Total cost	304,000	343,000	382,000

What would be the total cost in a budget that is flexed at the 77% level of activity?

O $330,300
O $370,300
O $373,300
O $377,300

12   The following extract is taken from the production cost budget for S Co:

Production (units)   4,000   6,000
Production cost ($)   11,100   12,900

The budget cost allowance for an activity level of 8,000 units is:

○ $7,200
○ $14,700
○ $17,200
○ $22,200

The following information relates to questions 13, 14 and 15

A&B Engineering Co produces a single product, the LSO, on an assembly line. The following production budgets represent the extremes of high and low volume of production likely to be encountered by the company over a 3 month period.

	Production of 4,000 units $	Production of 8,000 units $
Direct materials	80,000	160,000
Indirect materials	12,000	20,000
Direct labour	50,000	100,000
Power	18,000	24,000
Repairs	20,000	30,000
Supervision	20,000	36,000
Rent, insurance and rates	9,000	9,000

Supervision is a 'step function'. One supervisor is employed for all production levels up to and including 5,000 units. For higher levels of production an assistant supervisor ($16,000) is also required. For power, a minimum charge is payable on all production up to and including 6,000 units. For production above this level there is an additional variable charge based on the power consumed. Other variable and semi-variable costs are incurred evenly over the production range. The variable cost per unit of indirect materials is $2. The fixed cost of repairs is $10,000.

The table below will be used to prepare a set of flexible budgets for presentation to the production manager to cover levels of production over a period of three months of 4,000, 5,000, 6,000, 7,000 and 8,000 units.

	Budgets at different levels of activity				
	4,000 units	5,000 units	6,000 units	7,000 units	8,000 units
Direct materials					
Indirect materials	K	L	M	N	O
Direct labour					
Power	F	G	H	I	J
Repairs					
Supervision	A	B	C	D	E
Rent, insurance and rates					
Total					

13   What figures should be included at points A–E in the table above?

A [   ]

B [   ]

C [   ]

D [   ]

E [   ]

14   What figures should be included at points F–J in the table above?

F [   ]

G [   ]

H [   ]

I [   ]

J [   ]

15   What figures should be included at points K–O in the table above?

K [   ]

L [   ]

M [   ]

N [   ]

O [   ]

10 Budget preparation

1   Which of the following is not a functional budget?

- ○   Production budget
- ○   Distribution cost budget
- ○   Selling cost budget
- ○   Cash budget

2   If a company has no production resource limitations, in which order would the following budgets be prepared?

1   Material usage budget
2   Sales budget
3   Material purchase budget
4   Finished goods inventory budget
5   Production budget
6   Material inventory budget

○   5, 4, 1, 6, 3, 2
○   2, 4, 5, 1, 6, 3
○   2, 4, 5, 1, 3, 6
○   2, 5, 4, 1, 6, 3

---

3   Each unit of product Alpha requires 3 kg of raw material. Next month's production budget for product Alpha is as follows.

Opening inventories:
Raw materials   15,000 kg
Finished units of Alpha   2,000 units
Budgeted sales of Alpha   60,000 units
Planned closing inventories:
Raw materials   7,000 kg
Finished units of Alpha   3,000 units

The number of kilograms of raw materials that should be purchased next month is:

○   172,000
○   175,000
○   183,000
○   191,000

---

4   The following details have been extracted from the receivables collection records of C Co.

Invoices paid in the month after sale   60%
Invoices paid in the second month after sale   25%
Invoices paid in the third month after sale   12%
Bad debts   3%

Invoices are issued on the last day of each month. Customers paying in the month after sale are entitled to deduct a 2% settlement discount. Credit sales values for June to September are budgeted as follows.

June	July	August	September
$35,000	$40,000	$60,000	$45,000

The amount budgeted to be received from credit sales in September is:

○ $46,260
○ $49,480
○ $50,200
○ $50,530

5   RD Co is in the process of preparing its budgets for 20X2. The company produces and sells a single product, Z. The budgeted sales units for 20X2 are expected to be as follows:

July	Aug	Sep	Oct	Nov	Dec
6,250	7,000	7,500	7,750	8,000	7,500

The company expects to sell 7,000 units in January 20X3. It is company policy to hold a closing inventory balance of finished goods equal to 20% of the following month's sales.

The production budget for Quarter 4 is:

units

---

6   The following extracts from the DEF Co budget are available.

Year ended 30 June 20X9	$
Sales	1,135,600
Purchases	751,700
Closing inventory	113,500
Opening inventory	112,250
Opening receivables	163,525
Opening payables	113,550

DEF Co expects that receivables will increase by 12% and that payables will increase by 15% by the end of the year.

What is the budgeted cash receipts value from customers during the year?

$ [   ]

---

7   The following extracts from the DEF Co budget are available.

Year ended 30 June 20X9	$
Sales	1,135,600
Purchases	751,700
Closing inventory	113,500
Opening inventory	112,250
Opening receivables	163,525
Opening payables	113,550

DEF Co expects that receivables will increase by 12% and that payables will increase by 15% by the end of the year.

What is the profit mark-up as a percentage of cost of sales?

O   21%
O   31%
O   41%
O   51%

8   F Co has realised that it will have a temporary cash shortage before it receives the money for a very large order.

Which TWO of the following actions would be appropriate for F Co to take?

☐ Replace non-current assets

☐ Arrange an overdraft

☐ Pay suppliers early

☐ Implement better credit control procedures

☐ Increase inventory

---

9   The following details have been extracted from the receivables records of X:

Invoices paid in the month after sale	60%
Invoices paid in the second month after sale	20%
Invoices paid in the third month after sale	15%
Bad debts	5%

Credit sales for June to August 20X1 are budgeted as follows:

June	$100,000
July	$150,000
August	$130,000

Customers paying in the month after sale are entitled to deduct a 2% settlement discount. Invoices are issued on the last day of the month.

The amount budgeted to be received in September 20X1 from credit sales is:

○ $115,190
○ $116,750
○ $121,440
○ $123,000

---

10   RS is currently preparing the production budget for Product A and the material purchase budget for material X for the forthcoming year. Each unit of Product A requires 5 kg of material X.

The anticipated opening inventory for Product A is 5,000 units and the company wishes to increase the closing inventory by 30% by the end of the year. The anticipated opening inventory for material X is 50,000 kg and in order to avoid stock outs the required closing inventory has been increased to 60,000 kg.

The Sales Director has confirmed a sales requirement of 70,000 units of Product A.

What will be the purchases budget for material X?

○ 347,500 kg
○ 350,000 kg
○ 357,500 kg
○ 367,500 kg

11 The principal budget factor is the:

○   Factor that limits the activities of the organisation and is often the starting point in budget preparation

○   Budgeted revenue expected in a forthcoming period

○   Main budget into which all subsidiary budgets are consolidated

○   Overestimation of revenue budgets and underestimation of cost budgets, which operates as a safety factor against risk

12 Which TWO of the following items impact a cash budget?

☐   Funds from a bond issue
☐   Depreciation
☐   Bad debts written off
☐   Interest on a loan

The following information relates to questions 13, 14 and 15

Bertram Manufacturing Co produces a single product.

Sales of the product in the next four-week period are expected to be 280 units. At the beginning of the period an inventory level of 30 units is expected, although the budgeted closing inventory level is five units.

Each unit of the product requires 2 hours of grade O labour and 3 hours of grade R labour. Grade O labour is paid $15 per hour, whereas grade R labour receive a guaranteed weekly wage of $280.

Just one raw material is used in production of the product. A unit of the product requires 7 kg of raw material. The expected price per kg of the raw material is $50.

13 The budget production level is ⬚ units.

14 The materials usage budget is ⬚ kg, costing $ ⬚ .

15 The budgeted cost for grade O labour is $ ⬚ .

11 Variance analysis

1   T Co uses a standard costing system, with its material inventory account being maintained at standard cost. The following details have been extracted from the standard cost card in respect of direct materials:

8 kg @ $0.80/kg = $6.40 per unit

Budgeted production in April was 850 units.

The following details relate to actual materials purchased and issued to production during April when actual production was 870 units:

Materials purchased   8,200 kg costing $6,888
Materials issued to production   7,150 kg

The direct material price variance for April was:

○ $286 (A)
○ $286 (F)
○ $328 (A)
○ $328 (F)

2   T Co uses a standard costing system, with its material inventory account being maintained at standard cost. The following details have been extracted from the standard cost card in respect of direct materials:

8 kg @ $0.80/kg = $6.40 per unit

Budgeted production in April was 850 units.

The following details relate to actual materials purchased and issued to production during April when actual production was 870 units:

Materials purchased   8,200 kg costing $6,888
Materials issued to production   7,150 kg

The direct material usage variance for April was:

○ $152 (F)
○ $152 (A)
○ $159.60 (A)
○ $280 (A)

3   Barney Co expected to produce 200 units of its product, the Bone, in 20X3. In fact, 260 units were produced. The standard labour cost per unit was $70 (10 hours at a rate of $7 per hour). The actual labour cost was $18,600 and the labour force worked 2,200 hours, although they were paid for 2,300 hours.

What is the direct labour rate variance for Barney Co in 20X3?

○ $400 (A)
○ $2,500 (F)
○ $2,500 (A)
○ $3,200 (A)

4   Barney Co expected to produce 200 units of its product, the Bone, in 20X3. In fact, 260 units were produced. The standard labour cost per unit was $70 (10 hours at a rate of $7 per hour). The actual labour cost was $18,600 and the labour force worked 2,200 hours, although they were paid for 2,300 hours.

What is the direct labour efficiency variance for Barney Co in 20X3?

○ $400 (F)
○ $2,100 (F)
○ $2,800 (A)
○ $2,800 (F)

5   Trafalgar Co budgets to produce 10,000 units of product D12, each requiring 45 minutes of labour. Labour is charged at $20 per hour, and variable overheads at $15 per labour hour. During September 20X3, 11,000 units were produced. 8,000 hours of labour were paid at a total cost of $168,000. Variable overheads in September amounted to $132,000.

What is the correct labour efficiency variance for September 20X3?

- ○ $5,000 (A)
- ○ $5,000 (F)
- ○ $5,250 (F)
- ○ $10,000 (A)

6   Trafalgar Co budgets to produce 10,000 units of product D12, each requiring 45 minutes of labour. Labour is charged at $20 per hour, and variable overheads at $15 per labour hour. During September 20X3, 11,000 units were produced. 8,000 hours of labour were paid at a total cost of $168,000. Variable overheads in September amounted to $132,000.

What is the correct variable overhead expenditure variance for September 20X3?

- ○ $3,750 (F)
- ○ $4,125 (F)
- ○ $12,000 (A)
- ○ $12,000 (F)

7   A company manufactures a single product. The standard selling price is $70. The monthly budgeted contribution is $6,900, based on selling 230 units. In April the actual sales revenue was $15,200, when 200 units were sold.

The sales price variance in April was $ [   ] .

The sales volume contribution variance in April was $ [   ] .

8   Put the reasons for variances listed below into the correct place in the tables.

(a)

Variance	Favourable	Unfavourable
Material price		
Material usage		
Labour rate		

(b)

Variance	Favourable	Unfavourable
Labour efficiency		
Variable overhead expenditure		
Idle time		

A	Defective material
B	Lack of training of production workers
C	Machine breakdown
D	More economical use of non-material resources
E	Unforeseen discounts received
F	Wage rate increase

9   The budgeted material cost for Product Q is $20 per kg and 15 kg are budgeted per unit. In May the budgeted number of units of Q was 12,500. The actual number of units produced was 11,750 at a cost of $2,961,000 and 12 kg per unit were used. What is the total material variance?

○ $564,000 (F)
○ $564,000 (A)
○ $705,000 (A)
○ $705,000 (F)

10   The budgeted contribution for HMF Co for June was $290,000. The following variances occurred during the month.

	$	
Total direct labour variance	11,323	Favourable
Total variable overhead variance	21,665	Adverse
Selling price variance	21,875	Favourable
Fixed overhead volume variance	12,500	Adverse
Sales volume variance	36,250	Adverse
Total direct materials variance	6,335	Adverse

What was the actual contribution for the month?

○ $252,923
○ $258,948
○ $321,052
○ $327,077

11 During a period 17,500 labour hours were worked at a standard cost of $6.50 per hour. The labour efficiency variance was $7,800 favourable.

How many standard hours were produced?

- O 1,200
- O 16,300
- O 17,500
- O 18,700

12 Which of the following would help to explain an adverse direct material price variance?

1 The material purchased was of a higher quality than standard
2 A reduction in the level of purchases meant that expected bulk discounts were forgone
3 The standard price per unit of direct material was unrealistically high

- O All of them
- O 1 and 2 only
- O 2 and 3 only
- O 1 and 3 only

The following information relates to questions 13, 14 and 15

Extracts from V Co's records for June are as follows.

	Budget	Actual
Production	520 units	560 units
Variable production overhead cost	$3,120	$4,032
Labour hours worked	1,560	2,240

13 The variable production overhead total variance for June is:

- O $240 (A)
- O $672 (A)
- O $672 (F)
- O $912 (A)

14 The variable production overhead expenditure variance for June is:

- O $448 (F)
- O $448 (A)
- O $672 (A)
- O $912 (A)

15 The variable production overhead efficiency variance for June is:

- O $1,008 (A)
- O $1,120 (A)
- O $1,120 (F)
- O $1,360 (A)

12 Job and batch costing

1. Job 198 requires 380 active labour hours to complete. It is expected that there will be 5% idle time. The wage rate is $6 per hour. The labour cost of Job 198 is:

   ○ $2,166
   ○ $2,280
   ○ $2,394
   ○ $2,400

2. The following information relates to job 2468, which is being carried out by AB Co to meet a customer's order.

	Department A	Department B
Direct materials consumed	$5,000	$3,000
Direct labour hours	400 hours	200 hours
Direct labour rate per hour	$4	$5
Production o/head per direct lab hr	$4	$4
Administration and other overhead	20% of full production cost	
Profit margin	25% of sales price	

   What is the selling price to the customer for job 2468?

   ○ $16,250
   ○ $17,333
   ○ $19,500
   ○ $20,800

3. A company calculates the prices of jobs by adding overheads to the prime cost and adding 30% to total costs as profit. Job number Y256 was sold for $1,690 and incurred overheads of $694.

   What was the prime cost of the job?

   ○ $489
   ○ $606
   ○ $996
   ○ $1,300

4. In which of the following situation(s) will job costing normally be used?

   Select all that apply.

   ☐ Production is continuous
   ☐ Production of the product is of a relatively short duration
   ☐ Production relates to a single special order
   ☐ Production is over several accounting periods

5. A job requires 4,590 actual labour hours for completion and it is anticipated that there will be 10% idle time. If the wage rate is $8 per hour, the budgeted labour cost for the job is $ [   ] (to the nearest $).

6   Which of the following is a feature of job costing?

 ○   Production is carried out in accordance with the wishes of the customer.
 ○   Associated with continuous production of large volumes of low-cost items
 ○   Establishes the cost of services rendered
 ○   Costs are charged over the units produced in the period.

---

7   JW Co is planning to launch a new wall paint for bathrooms and kitchens called WR1. This will be manufactured in batches of 100,000 cans.

The following cost estimates have been produced per batch of WR1.

Paint WR1 cost estimates	$
Direct material per batch	103,000
Direct labour per batch	105,000
Variable production overheads per batch	84,000
Fixed production overheads per batch	34,000
Administration, selling and distribution costs per batch	41,000
Total costs	367,000

Calculate the estimated full absorption cost of one BATCH of WR1.

$ [   ]

Calculate the estimated marginal production cost of one CAN of WR1 (round to 2 decimal places).

$ [   ]

---

8   Which THREE of the following are contained in a typical batch cost?

 ☐   Actual material cost

 ☐   Actual manufacturing overheads

 ☐   Absorbed manufacturing overheads

 ☐   Actual labour cost

---

9   AL Co operates a job costing system. The company's standard net profit margin is 20% of sales value.

The estimated costs for job B124 are as follows.

Direct materials   3 kg @ $5 per kg
Direct labour   4 hours @ $9 per hour

Production overheads are budgeted to be $240,000 for the period, to be recovered on the basis of a total of 30,000 labour hours.

Other overheads, related to selling, distribution and administration, are budgeted to be $150,000 for the period. They are to be recovered on the basis of the total budgeted production cost of $750,000 for the period.

The price to be quoted for job B124 is $ [   ] (to the nearest cent).

BPP
LEARNING
MEDIA

10   A small management consultancy has prepared the following information.

Overhead absorption rate per consulting hour	$12.50
Salary cost per consulting hour (senior)	$20.00
Salary cost per consulting hour (junior)	$15.00

The firm adds 40% to total cost to arrive at a selling price.

Assignment number 652 took 86 hours of a senior consultant's time and 220 hours of junior time.

What price should be charged for assignment number 652?

- ○ $7,028
- ○ $8,845
- ○ $12,383
- ○ $14,742

11   A small management consultancy has prepared the following information.

Overhead absorption rate per consulting hour	$12.50
Salary cost per consulting hour (senior)	$20.00
Salary cost per consulting hour (junior)	$15.00

The firm adds 40% to total cost to arrive at a selling price.

During a period 3,000 consulting hours were charged out in the ratio of 1 senior to 3 junior hours. Overheads were exactly as budgeted.

What was the total gross margin for the period?

- ○ $34,500
- ○ $57,500
- ○ $86,250
- ○ $120,750

12   Which TWO of the following are characteristics of job costing?

- ☐ Customer-driven production
- ☐ Complete production possible within a single accounting period
- ☐ Homogeneous products
- ☐ The cost unit consists of a separate group of units

The following information relates to questions 13, 14 and 15

A firm makes special assemblies to customers' orders and uses job costing.

The data for a period are:

	Job number AA10 $	Job number BB15 $	Job number CC20 $
Opening WIP	26,800	42,790	0
Material added in period	17,275	0	18,500
Labour for period	14,500	3,500	24,600

The budgeted overheads for the period were $126,000.

---

13   What overhead should be added to job number CC20 for the period?

  O $65,157
  O $69,290
  O $72,761
  O $126,000

---

14   Job number BB15 was completed and delivered during the period and the firm wishes to earn 33.3% profit on sales.

What is the selling price of job number BB15?

  O $69,435
  O $75,521
  O $84,963
  O $258,435

---

15   What was the approximate value of closing work in progress at the end of the period?

  O $58,575
  O $101,675
  O $217,323
  O $227,675

---

13 Performance measures and service costing

1   State which of the following are characteristics of service costing.

  1 High levels of indirect costs as a proportion of total costs
  2 Use of composite cost units
  3 Tangible units of production

  O 1 only
  O 1 and 2 only
  O 2 only
  O 2 and 3 only

2   Which of the following would be appropriate cost units for a transport business?

1   Cost per tonne-kilometre
2   Fixed cost per kilometre
3   Maintenance cost of each vehicle per kilometre

○   1 only
○   1 and 2 only
○   1 and 3 only
○   1, 2 and 3

3   Which of the following organisations should NOT be advised to use service costing?

○   Distribution service
○   Hospital
○   Maintenance division of a manufacturing company
○   A light engineering company

4   Calculate the most appropriate unit cost for a distribution division of a multinational company using the following information.

Miles travelled   636,500
Tonnes carried   2,479
Number of drivers   20
Hours worked by drivers   35,520
Tonne-miles carried   375,200
Costs incurred $562,800

○ $0.88
○ $1.50
○ $15.84
○ $28,140

5   Which of the following are characteristics of service costing?

Select all that apply.

☐   High levels of indirect costs as a proportion of total cost
☐   Perishability
☐   Use of composite cost units
☐   Homogeneity

6   Which THREE of the following would be appropriate cost units for a private taxi company?

☐   Vehicle cost per passenger-kilometre
☐   Maintenance cost per vehicle per kilometre
☐   Fixed cost per passenger
☐   Fuel cost per kilometre

7 Which THREE of the following would be suitable cost units for a hospital?

☐ Patient/day
☐ Operating theatre hour
☐ Ward
☐ X-ray department
☐ Outpatient visit

8 Match up the following services with their typical cost units.

Service	Cost unit
Hotels	☐
Education	☐
Hospitals	☐
Catering organisations	☐

○ Meal served
○ Patient day
○ Full-time student
○ Occupied bed-night

9 If sales are $25,500, and cost of sales are $21,250, what is the gross profit percentage?

○ 16.67%
○ 20.00%
○ 83.33%
○ 120.00%

10 Your company's statement of profit or loss for the year ended 30 September 20X8 showed the following:

	$'000
Net profit before interest and tax	1,200
Interest	200
	1,000
Corporation tax	400
Retained profit for the year	600

The statement of financial position at 30 September 20X8 showed the following capital:

	$'000
Share capital	8,000
Retained earnings	1,200
	9,200
10% loan stock	2,000
	11,200

What is the return on capital employed for the year ended 30 September 20X8?

- ○ 5.88%
- ○ 13.04%
- ○ 10.71%
- ○ 10.87%

11   In not for profit businesses and state-run entities, a value-for-money audit can be used to measure performance. It covers three key areas: economy, efficiency and effectiveness. Which of the following could be used to describe effectiveness in this context?

- ○ Avoiding waste of inputs
- ○ Achieving agreed targets
- ○ Achieving a given level of profit
- ○ Obtaining suitable quality inputs at the lowest price

12   A government body uses measures based upon the 'three Es' to the measure value for money generated by a publicly funded hospital. It considers the most important performance measure to be 'cost per successfully treated patient'.

Which of the three E's best describes the above measure?

- ○ Economy
- ○ Effectiveness
- ○ Efficiency
- ○ Externality

The following information relates to questions 13, 14 and 15

Florrie Co's summarised results for the last two years are shown below.

	20X1	20X2
	$'000	$'000
Sales	80,000	100,000
Gross profit	22,000	30,000
Net profit	12,000	16,000
Capital employed	60,000	80,000

13   Calculate the net profit margin percentage for both 20X1 and 20X2.

20X1   20X2

[   ] %   [   ] %

14   Calculate the return on capital employed (ROCE) percentage for both 20X1 and 20X2.

20X1   20X2

[   ] %   [   ] %

BPP LEARNING MEDIA

15   Calculate the asset turnover for both 20X1 and 20X2 to two decimal places.

20X1   *20X2*

[   ] %   [   ] %

14 Cost bookkeeping

1   A firm operates an integrated cost and financial accounting system. The accounting entries for indirect wages incurred would be:

	Debit	Credit
O	Wages control account	Overhead control account
O	Work in progress account	Wages control account
O	Overhead control account	Wages control account
O	Wages control account	Work in progress account

2   X Co has recorded the following wages costs for direct production workers for November.

	$
Basic pay	70,800
Overtime premium	2,000
Holiday pay	500
Gross wages incurred	73,300

The overtime was not worked for any specific job.

The accounting entries for these wages costs would be:

		Debit $	Credit $
O	Work in progress account	72,800	
	Overhead control account	500	
	Wages control account		73,300
O	Work in progress account	70,800	
	Overhead control account	2,500	
	Wages control account		73,300
O	Wages control account	73,300	
	Work in progress account		70,800
	Overhead control account		2,500
O	Wages control account	73,300	
	Work in progress account		72,800
	Overhead control account		500

3   The wages control account for A Co for February is shown below.

WAGES CONTROL ACCOUNT

	$		$
Bank	128,400	Work in progress control	79,400
Balance c/d	12,000	Production overhead control	61,000
	140,400		140,400
		Balance b/d	12,000

Which of the following statements about wages for February is not correct?

○   Wages paid during February amounted to $128,400.
○   Wages for February were prepaid by $12,000.
○   Direct wages cost incurred during February amounted to $79,400.
○   Indirect wages cost incurred during February amounted to $61,000.

4   When a standard cost bookkeeping system is used and the actual price paid for raw materials exceeds the standard price, the double entry to record this is:

	Debit	*Credit*
○	Raw material control account	Raw material price variance account
○	Work in progress control account	Raw material price variance account
○	Raw material price variance account	Raw material control account
○	Raw material price variance account	Work in progress control account

5   A firm uses an integrated standard cost bookkeeping system. The double entry for a favourable labour efficiency variance is:

	Debit	*Credit*
○	Labour efficiency variance account	Wages control account
○	Work in progress control account	Labour efficiency variance account
○	Wages control account	Labour efficiency variance account
○	Labour efficiency variance account	Work in progress control account

6   A firm uses standard costing and an integrated accounting system. The double entry for a favourable material usage variance is:

	Debit	*Credit*
○	Suppliers control account	Material usage variance account
○	Material usage variance account	Stores control account
○	Work in progress control account	Material usage variance account
○	Material usage variance account	Work in progress control account

7   The bookkeeping entries in a standard cost system when the actual price for raw materials purchased is less than the standard price are:

	Debit	Credit	No entry in this account
Raw materials control account			
WIP control account			
Raw material price variance account			

8   A firm uses an integrated standard cost bookkeeping system. The double entry for a favourable labour rate variance is:

	Debit	Credit
O	Labour rate variance account	Wages control account
O	Work in progress control account	Labour rate variance account
O	Labour rate variance account	Work in progress control account
O	Wages control account	Labour rate variance account

9   A firm uses an integrated standard cost bookkeeping system. The double entry for an adverse material usage variance is:

	Debit	Credit
O	Material usage variance account	Work in progress control account
O	Material usage variance account	Stores ledger control account
O	Work in progress control account	Material usage variance account
O	Stores ledger control account	Material usage variance account

10   A company operates an integrated accounting system. The accounting entries for the factory cost of finished production would be:

	Debit	Credit
O	Work in progress control account	Finished goods control account
O	Costing statement of profit or loss	Finished goods control account
O	Finished goods control account	Work in progress control account
O	Cost of sales account	Finished goods control account

11   In an integrated cost and financial accounting system, the accounting entries at the end of the period for factory overhead over-absorbed would be (tick the correct boxes):

	Debit	Credit	No entry in this account
Overhead control account			
Work in progress account			
Statement of profit or loss			

12   A firm operates an integrated cost and financial accounting system.

The accounting entries for an issue of direct materials to production would be

- O   DR work in progress control account; CR stores control account
- O   DR finished goods account; CR stores control account
- O   DR stores control account; CR work in progress control account
- O   DR cost of sales account; CR work in progress control account

The following information relates to questions 13, 14 and 15

A manufacturing company uses an integrated accounting system. The production overhead absorption rate is $3 per direct labour hour. Production overhead incurred last period was $85,000 and 27,000 direct labour hours were worked. Other information was as follows:

	$
Opening inventory	18,500
Closing inventory	16,100
Deliveries from suppliers	142,000
Returns to suppliers	2,300
Cost of indirect materials issued	25,200

13　The accounting entries to record the absorption of production overhead for the period would be:

	Debit		Credit	
O	Work in progress account	$85,000	Overhead control account	$85,000
O	Finished goods account	$81,000	Overhead control account	$81,000
O	Work in progress account	$81,000	Overhead control account	$81,000
O	Overhead control account	$81,000	Work in progress account	$81,000

14　The accounting entries to record the under or over absorption of production overhead for the period would be:

	Debit		Credit	
O	Statement of profit or loss	$4,000	Overhead control account	$4,000
O	Overhead control account	$4,000	Statement of profit or loss	$4,000
O	Work in progress account	$4,000	Overhead control account	$4,000
O	Overhead control account	$4,000	Work in progress account	$4,000

15　How is the issue of direct materials recorded in the cost accounts?

			$	$
O	Debit	Stores ledger control account	119,200	
	Credit	Work in progress control account		119,200
O	Debit	Work in progress control account	119,200	
	Credit	Stores ledger control account		119,200
O	Debit	Stores ledger control account	116,900	
	Credit	Work in progress control account		116,900
O	Debit	Work in progress control account	116,900	
	Credit	Stores ledger control account		116,900

15 Risk and probability

1   Next year, sales may rise, fall or remain the same as this year, with the following respective probabilities: 0.56, 0.23 and 0.21.

What is the probability of sales remaining the same (A) or falling (B) (to 2 decimal places)?

Probability of A or B occurring = [   ]

---

2   In a student survey, 40% of the students are male and 80% are CIMA candidates.

What is the probability (to 2 decimal places) that a student chosen at random is either female or a CIMA candidate?

[   ]

---

3   A sales representative visits two independent firms – L and W. The probability of making a sale at L is 0.3 and the probability of making a sale at W is 0.4.

What is the probability (to 2 decimal places) of making no sale at all?

[   ]

---

4   A firm employs three sales staff and the probabilities that they will make a sale on a given day are 0.4, 0.45 and 0.5 respectively. Each person never makes more than one sale per day and acts independently of the others.

Find the probability that at least one sale is made on a particular day (to 3 decimal places).

[   ]

---

5   A pet food company has developed a low-fat dog food designed to make overweight dogs lose weight. In field tests on 1,000 dogs, some dogs ate the new food and some a normal dog food. The results of the tests were as follows.

	Given normal food	Given low-fat food
Lost weight	250	200
No weight loss	250	300

What is the probability that a dog has lost weight, given that it received low-fat food (to 2 decimal places)?

[   ]

---

6   Which of the following statements are true about an expected value?

1   It is a weighted average based on probabilities.
2   It is the sum of the probabilities multiplied by the outcomes.

○   Statement 1 only
○   Statement 1 and 2
○   Neither statement
○   Statement 2 only

---

7 Which of the following is not a limitation of an expected value (EV)?

○ An EV is inappropriate for one-off decisions.
○ An EV is based on probabilities that may be unreliable.
○ An EV is inappropriate if decisions are being constantly repeated.
○ EV ignores risk.

8 A project may result in profits of $15,000 or $20,000, or in a loss of $5,000. The probabilities of each profit are 0.2, 0.5 and 0.3 respectively.

What is the expected profit (to the nearest $)?

$ [   ]

9 A company must decide between two projects – Project Alpha and Project Beta. The profits that might be generated from each project are as follows.

Project Alpha		Project Beta	
Probability	Profit	Probability	Profit
0.5	$50,000	0.6	$60,000
0.5	$20,000	0.4	$10,000

Which project should the company choose?

○ Project Alpha
○ Project Beta

10 A project is thought to have a 0.6 probability of making a profit of $3,000 and a 0.4 probability of making a profit of $1,500.

Find the change in expected profit if the probabilities actually turn out to be 0.55 and 0.45 respectively (to the nearest $).

$ [   ]

11 A sales representative makes calls to three separate unrelated customers. The chance of making a sale at any one of them is 80%. The probability (to the nearest percent) that a sale is made on the third call only is

[   ] %.

12 A company sells much of its output on credit. It employs a credit rating agency and experience shows that of those customers rated a good credit risk, 90% settle their debts without difficulty. The company does not extend credit to those rated a bad credit risk.

The credit rating agency does not have information on all would-be customers, however. Experience shows that of those customers who are given credit without a check from the credit rating agency, 80% settle their debts without difficulty. 60% of customers are not checked by the credit rating agency.

The probability that a customer who defaults was actually checked by a credit rating agency is (to 2 decimal places):

[   ]

The following information relates to questions 13, 14 and 15

High Street Shoe Store has analysed the expenditure habits of a random sample of 500 of its customers and produced the following table showing the number of customers in each category:

	Age of customer		
	Under 21	21 and over	Total
Expenditure			
Under $25	55	205	260
$25 to $50	125	80	205
Over $50	10	25	35
	190	310	500

13   The probability that a customer is aged under 21 and spent between $25 and $50 is [   ].

State your answer to 2 decimal places.

14   If a customer is aged under 21, the probability that he spent between $25 and $50 is [   ].

State your answer to 2 decimal places.

15   The probability that a customer who spent between $25 and $50 is aged under 21 is [   ].

State your answer to 2 decimal places.

16   The following decision tree shows four decision options: 1, 2, 3 and 4.

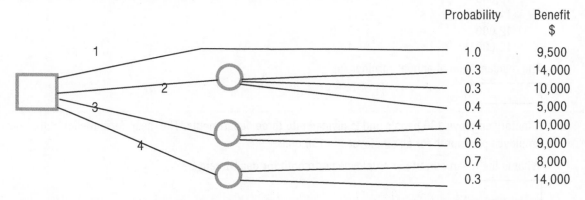

Probability	Benefit $
1.0	9,500
0.3	14,000
0.3	10,000
0.4	5,000
0.4	10,000
0.6	9,000
0.7	8,000
0.3	14,000

Using the expected value rule, which choice should be made so as to optimise the expected benefit?

○   Choice 1
○   Choice 2
○   Choice 3
○   Choice 4

16 Averages and the normal distribution

1   A normal distribution has a mean of 75 and a variance of 25.

    The upper quartile of this distribution is therefore:

    ○   58.25
    ○   71.65
    ○   78.35
    ○   91.75

2   Sample 1: 2, 5, 5, 12
    Sample 2: 1, 3, 5, 8, 8

    Which of the following statistics has the same value in both samples?

    ○   Arithmetic mean
    ○   Standard deviation
    ○   Median
    ○   Mode

3   In a supermarket, the number of employees and the annual earnings per employee are shown as follows.

Annual earnings $	Number employed
6,000	3
7,000	5
10,000	3
11,000	1
12,000	2
15,000	1

    The median value of annual earnings is:

    [   ]

4   A factory employs 100 people and is divided into three departments. The mean (arithmetic) output per employee per month for all employees is 139 units.

    What is the mean output per employee per month for department 2?

    [   ]

Department	No of employees in department	Mean output per employee per month Units
1	54	130
2	?	?
3	24	140

5   The weights of three items – A, B and C – vary independently and have the following means and standard deviations.

	Mean weight kg	Variance
A	120	400
B	100	400
C	80	100

The three items are sold together in a single packet.

What is the mean weight of a packet of one unit each of A, B and C, and the standard deviation of the weights of packets?

	Mean weight kg	Standard deviation kg
O	100	30
O	100	900
O	300	30
O	300	900

6   On one particular checkout in a supermarket, the service time has an arithmetic mean of 5 minutes and a standard deviation of 1 minute. The coefficient of variation will be:

- O   50%
- O   20%
- O   5%
- O   2%

7   The following has been calculated for a frequency distribution.

$\Sigma(f) = $ 50
$\Sigma(fx) = $ 1,610
$\Sigma(fx^2) = $ 61,250

The value of the standard deviation (to 1 decimal place) is [   ].

8   The number of rejects from 50 samples of the same size is as follows:

Number of rejects in each sample	Number of samples (frequency of reject)
0	5
1	10
2	10
3	20
4	5
5	0

The arithmetic mean number of rejects per sample is:

- O   2.2
- O   2.4
- O   3
- O   20

9   The number of daily complaints to a railway company has an average (arithmetic mean) of 12 and a standard deviation of 3 complaints. The coefficient of variation, measured as a percentage, is therefore:

○   0.25%
○   4%
○   25%
○   400%

10   Production of aluminium tubes is normally distributed with a mean length of 50 cm and a standard deviation of 5 cm. The percentage of tubes at least 57 cm long is closest to:

○   8%
○   42%
○   58%
○   92%

11   The weight of a product is normally distributed with a mean of 400 g, 39% of total production falls within the weight range 350 g to 450 g. What is the standard deviation?

○   98 g
○   38 g
○   49 g
○   19 g

12   A normal distribution has a mean of 55 and a variance of 14.44. The probability of a score of 59 or more is approximately:

○   0.15
○   0.35
○   0.50
○   0.65

The following information relates to questions 13, 14 and 15

The following times have been recorded for dealing with customer queries.

30, 35, 31, 25, 25, 31, 23, 31, 30

13   What is the median time?

14   What is the mode time?

15   What is the mean time?

16   A histogram uses a set of rectangles to represent a grouped frequency table. To be correctly presented, the histogram must show the relationship of the rectangles to the frequencies by reference to the:

○   Height
○   Area
○   Width
○   Diagonal of each rectangle

17   The following table shows the typical salary of part qualified management accountants in five different regions of England.

Area	Typical salary
	$
South-east	21,500
Midlands	20,800
North-east	18,200
North-west	17,500
South-west	16,700

The best diagram to draw to highlight the differences between areas is

○   A pie diagram
○   A multiple bar chart
○   A percentage component bar chart
○   A simple bar chart

18   In a pie chart, printing costs for the year are represented by 60° and the total costs for the year are $630,000. What are the printing costs for the year?

$ _____ (Give your answer to the nearest whole $)

17 Investment appraisal

1   Which is worth most, at present values, assuming an annual rate of interest of 8%?

○ $1,200 in exactly one year from now
○ $1,400 in exactly two years from now
○ $1,600 in exactly three years from now
○ $1,800 in exactly four years from now

2   A project has a net present value (NPV) of $22 at 9% and an NPV of –$4 at 10%.

What is the internal rate of return (IRR) for the project?

○   9.15%
○   9.85%
○   10.15%
○   10.85%

3   What is the yardstick for acceptance of projects when using the net present value method?

      O   Accept if a profit is made

      O   Accept if the present value of future cash flows is positive

      O   Accept if payback occurs within a reasonable timeframe

      O   Accept if the discount rate that achieves a breakeven return is greater than the company's cost of capital

---

4   A company has decided to lease a machine. Six annual payments of $8,000 will be made, with the first payment on receipt of the machine. Below is an extract from an annuity table:

Year	Annuity factor 10%
1	0.909
2	1.736
3	2.487
4	3.170
5	3.791
6	4.355

What is the present value of the lease payments at an interest rate of 10%?

      O $30,328

      O $34,840

      O $38,328

      O $48,000

---

5   What is the present value of ten annual payments of $700, the first paid immediately and discounted at 8%, giving your answer to the nearest $?

      O $4,697

      O $1,050

      O $4,435

      O $5,073

---

6   A machine has an investment cost of $60,000 at time 0. The present values (at time 0) of the expected net cash inflows from the machine over its useful life are:

Discount rate %	Present value of cash inflows $
10	64,600
15	58,200
20	52,100

What is the internal rate of return (IRR) of the machine investment?

      O   Below 10%

      O   Between 10% and 15%

      O   Between 15% and 20%

      O   Over 20%

---

7   An investment project has a positive net present value (NPV) of $7,222 when its cash flows are discounted at the cost of capital of 10% per annum. Net cash inflows from the project are expected to be $18,000 per annum for five years. The cumulative discount (annuity) factor for five years at 10% is 3.791.

What is the investment at the start of the project?

O $61,016
O $68,238
O $75,460
O $82,778

8   Which of the following statements about payback method of investment appraisal are true?

1   It is a fairly complex technique and not easy to understand
2   It ignores the time value of money
3   It takes account of all cash flows

O   None of the statements are true
O   All of the statements are true
O   Statement 2 only
O   Statement 3 only

9   Which of the following are problems in using net present value to appraise an investment?

1   The difficulty of estimating future cash flows
2   The difficulty of selecting an appropriate discount rate
3   It does not take account of inflation.
4   The concept of net present value is difficult for non-accountants to understand.

O   1 and 2 only
O   1, 2 and 3 only
O   1, 2 and 4 only
O   1, 2, 3 and 4

10   An investment has a net present value of $35,000 at 2% and $15,000 at 8%.

What is the approximate internal rate of return?

O   10.5%
O   12.5%
O   9.5%
O   8.0%

11   A project has an initial outflow of $12,000 followed by six equal annual cash inflows, commencing in one year's time. The payback period is exactly four years. The cost of capital is 12% per year.

What is the project's net present value (to the nearest $)?

O $333
O   −$2,899
O   −$3,778
O   −$5,926

12   Guild Co is considering purchasing a new machine. The relevant cash flows are:

	$
Cost	125,000
Cash inflows	
Year 1	35,500
Year 2	45,500
Year 3	52,000
Year 4	27,000
Total	160,000

Calculate the payback period of the new machine.

- ○   2 years and 6 months
- ○   2 years and 8 months
- ○   2 years and 10 months
- ○   3 years exactly

The following information relates to questions 13, 14 and 15

Livid Co has a payback period of 3 years and is considering investing in the following project. The initial investment required is $800,000. Cash flows occur evenly throughout the year and the cost of capital is 10%.

Year	*Project* *Cash inflow*
	$
1	250,000
2	350,000
3	400,000
4	200,000
5	150,000
6	150,000

13   What is the payback period of the project?

- ○   2 years and 2 months
- ○   2 years and 4 months
- ○   2 years and 5 months
- ○   2 years and 6 months

14   What is the net present value (NPV) of the project?

$ [   ]

15   The NPV of the project using a 20% discount rate is $89,700 and the NPV is –$77,024 using a discount rate of 30%. What is the internal rate of return to one decimal place?

[   ] %

16   Using the picklist, indicate whether the information below relates to the payback period, net present value (NPV) or internal rate of return (IRR).

Ignores the time value of money	▼
Discount rate that gives a NPV of zero	▼
Accept project if appraisal method gives a positive figure	▼
Most important investment criterion	▼

Picklist

NPV
IRR
Payback

Answers

1 Introduction to management accounting

1   The correct answer is: Having skills, knowledge and expertise

'Having skills, knowledge and expertise' features in the IFAC definition of the role of the Professional Accountant in Business.

https://www.ifac.org/publications-resources/roles-and-domain-professional-accountant-business PDF p2

2   The correct answer is: Ensuring that each member complies with CIMA's regulations

It is the responsibility of each student and member to make sure they comply with the regulations.

3   The correct answer is: Planning, control and decision making only

Management information is used for planning, control and decision making.

4   The correct answer is: Internal managers

Management accounts are produced for the internal managers of an organisation. The other groups of people would use the financial accounts of an organisation.

5   The correct answer is: Stakeholders

Stakeholders can include shareholders, customers, suppliers, employees or anyone that could be affected by the company internally or externally.

6   The correct answer is: None of the above

Management accountants can work in a variety of roles and also across a range of departments.

7   The correct answers are:

CIMA was established over 90 years ago. CIMA members and students must comply with the CIMA code of ethics. CIMA members work in all areas of business.

For a detailed history of CIMA, students can visit the global CIMA homepage in the 'about us' section.

8   The correct answer is: Implementing corporate governance

The role of a management accountant involves assisting management with planning, control and decision making to achieve the objectives of the business. The management accountant produces information to help plan business operations at the start of the year, control and monitor performance during the year and in the production of financial statements at the year end.

Corporate governance, ie the rules and practices by which the company is run, is the responsibility of the board of directors.

9   The correct answer is: Managerial

Monthly variance reports are an example of managerial management information.

10   The correct answer is: Management accounting systems provide information for the use of decision makers within an organisation

Financial accounting systems provide information for legal requirements, shareholders and tax authorities. Management accounting systems provide information specifically for the use of decision makers (managers) within the organisation.

BPP LEARNING MEDIA

11   The correct answer is: Management

Management is responsible for planning, control and decision making in a business.

12   The correct answer is: Complexity

Good information should be as simple as possible – remember the mnemonic ACCURATE. Accurate, Complete, Cost-beneficial, User-targeted, Relevant, Authoritative, Timely, Easy to use.

13   The correct answers are:

Stewardship builds trust
Communication provides insight that is influential
Impact on value is analysed
Information is relevant

The Global Management Accounting Principles were created by the AICPA (American Institute of CPAs) and CIMA.

14   The correct answers are:

To help organisations plan for and source the information needed for creating strategy and tactics for execution

To actively manage relationships and resources so that the financial and non-financial assets, reputation and value of the organisation are protected

To simulate different scenarios that demonstrate the cause-and-effect relationships between inputs and outcomes

To drive better decisions about strategy and its execution

15   The correct answer is: Both statements are true.

16   The correct answers are:

	Management accounting	Financial accounting
Information focuses on the needs of internal management	✓	
Information can be presented in any format	✓	
Information relates to both the future and the past	✓	
Information is specified by law		✓

17   The correct answer is: Less control over the finance function

Advantages and disadvantages of business process outsourcing are:

Advantages	Disadvantages
Reduced costs (eg fixed salary costs saved)	Over-reliance on the external supplier
Increased capacity of the organisation's finance team (where only routine functions are outsourced)	Less control over the finance function
Access to specialists	Potential risk to confidential information
	Potential reduced quality of information

18   The correct answers are: Preparation of cash budgets and Helping with planning within the organisation.

      Checking the accuracy of year end financial statements is done by the auditor.

      Preparation of the statement of profit or loss account is done by financial accountants rather than management accountants.

19   The correct answer is: Operational tasks are short term in timescale

      Strategic tasks are unstructured. Tactical information is mostly internal. Operational plans are implemented by low level management.

20   The correct answer is: Seb: Operational information Jai: Strategic information

      Operational information deals with matters relevant to the immediate term or short term and it is detailed and about the manager's own department. Seb is a supervisor, not a manager, and this should have helped you to decide that he is looking at operational information rather than management information.

      Jai is dealing with strategic information. Strategic information is derived from internal or external sources and is relevant to the long term (eg relevant to an organisation's commercial strategy). A good example of this is long term finance.

2 Costing

1   The correct answer is: Items 2 and 3 only

      It would be appropriate to use the cost per invoice processed and the cost per supplier account for control purposes. Therefore items 2 and 3 are suitable cost units.

      Postage cost, item 1, is an expense of the department, therefore this option is not a suitable cost unit.

      If you selected the other options you were probably rushing ahead and not taking care to read all the options. Items 2 and 3 are suitable cost units, but neither of them are the only suitable suggestions.

2   The correct answer is: Cost of transporting raw materials from the supplier's premises

      This option is a part of the cost of direct materials.

      The second and fourth options are production overheads. The third option is a selling and distribution expense.

3   The correct answers are: It is not a cash cost. It is part of production overheads.

      Depreciation is the allocation of the depreciable amount of an asset over its useful life. No cash is exchanged. The depreciation on production equipment is an indirect expense incurred in the factory and is therefore included in production overheads.

4   The correct answers are: Wood used to make a chair. Metal used for the legs of a chair. Fabric to cover the seat of a chair.

      The salary of the sales director is a selling overhead and the depreciation of the delivery vehicle is a distribution overhead. The other costs are direct costs.

5   The correct answer is: An administration cost

      Audit fees cannot be allocated under any of the other costs as they are for the whole company, therefore it must be an admin cost.

6   The correct answer is: Functions or locations for which costs are ascertained

A cost centre is a production or service location, a function, an activity or an item of equipment for which costs are accumulated, eg a canteen within a company.

7   The correct answer is: The cost of ingredients

Ingredients would be classified as the raw material and not a production overhead.

8   The correct answer is: Direct labour

A direct cost is one which can be attributed to a cost unit (final product), while an indirect cost is incurred as a lump sum and cannot be attributed to a cost unit. A production manager's salary is usually an indirect cost as it is not attributable per unit, as he is responsible for supervising production activities across different products within the factory. However, in cases where the factory produces just one product, the full salary of the manager can be attributed to that product and will therefore be classified as a direct labour cost.

9   The correct answer is: Assembly line worker

A direct cost is one which can be attributed in full to a cost unit, ie to the final product produced. An assembly line worker works within the assembly line cost centre and is directly involved in making cars – his salary can be attributed in full to the cars produced and is therefore a direct labour cost.

The cook, stores assistant and factory accountant support the production facilities and are not directly involved in producing the cars (the final product) and thus their salaries are considered to be indirect labour costs.

10   The correct answer is: A cost that can be influenced by its budget holder

Controllable costs are items of expenditure that can be directly influenced by a given manager within a given time span.

11   The correct answers are: Avoidable cost. Future cost. Differential cost.

Avoidable costs are relevant because they get affected by the decision, eg we are currently paying rent and if we were to buy or build our own workplace, this rent would become a cost saving (avoidable cost/relevant cost).

If there are any future costs incurred due to a decision we make, then they come under relevant costs of the decision. (However future committed costs are irrelevant.)

For example, the salary of a new supervisor recruited specifically for the new building is a future relevant cost, however if we were to recruit a new supervisor to start in six months' time (future) and we were to use him in the new project then his salary becomes irrelevant because it is a future committed cost.

This is another name for incremental costs (eg at the moment we are paying a rent of $6,000 but if we had to pay rent of $8,500, the differential cost of $2,500 is relevant to the decision of expanding).

A sunk cost is a cost that has been incurred in the past. It is irrelevant to any decision that is being made now.

A committed cost is a future cash flow that will be incurred anyway, regardless of the decision taken now. It is therefore not a relevant cost.

12 The correct answers are:

Cost item	Cost type
Carbon for racquet heads	Direct material
Office stationery	Administration costs
Wages of employees stringing racquets	Direct labour
Supervisors' salaries	Indirect labour
Advertising stand at badminton tournaments	Selling and distribution costs

13 The correct answer is: $4,500

In a relevant costing question like this, if materials are regularly used then they are to be replaced.

Hence we have to purchase them from outside. The replacement cost here is $4,500 which should be considered as the relevant cost for the job.

14 The correct answer is: $375

Skilled labour capacity = 75 hrs
Requirement   = 100 hrs
Relevant cost   = 25 hrs @ rate of ($525/35hrs) = 25 hrs × $15 = $375

Unskilled labour is not a relevant cost as there is spare capacity.

15 The correct answer is: The overheads should be excluded because they are not incremental costs.

The overhead costs will be incurred regardless of whether the job goes ahead so they are not incremental. Sunk costs are past costs and the overheads are not past costs.

3 Cost behaviour

1 The correct answer is: Be constant per unit of output

Variable costs are conventionally deemed to increase or decrease in direct proportion to changes in output. Options 2 and 4 imply a changing unit rate, which does not comply with this convention. The third option relates to a fixed cost.

2 The correct answer is: Electricity bills made up of a standing charge and a variable charge

The depicted cost has a basic fixed element which is payable even at zero activity. A variable element is then added at a constant rate as activity increases.

Graphs for the other options would look like this:

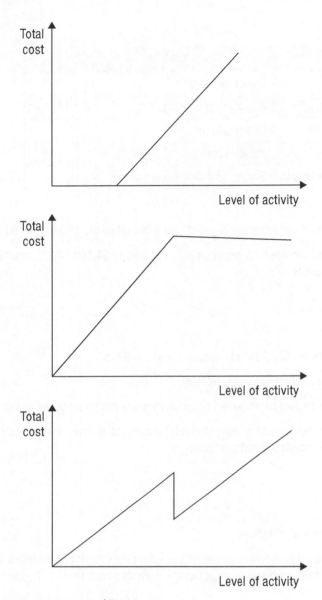

3   The correct answer is: $5,100

	Unit	$
High output	1,000	18,300
Low output	700	13,500
Variable cost of	400	4,800

Variable cost per unit $4,800/$400 = $12 per unit

Fixed costs = $18,300 – ($12 × 1,100) = $5,100

Therefore the correct answer is C.

The first option is the total cost for an activity of 700 units.

The second option is the total variable cost for 1,100 units (1,100 × $12).

The fourth option is the difference between the costs incurred at the two activity levels recorded.

4   The correct answer is: $0.50

Variable cost for 340 guest-nights = $570 − $400 = $170

Variable cost per guest-night = $170/340 = $0.50

5   The correct answer is: Discounts are received on additional purchases of material when certain quantities are purchased.

If bonuses are paid at higher production levels then the steepness of the gradient would increase as output increases.

6   The correct answer is: $17,625

	Patients	Cost
		$
Low	(650)	(17,125)
High	1,260	18,650
	610	1,525

Obtain variable cost per patient as $1,525/610 = $2.5 per patient.
Therefore fixed cost is $17,125 − $1,625 ($2.50 × 650) = $15,500.
Variable cost for 850 patients would be $2.50 × 850 = $2,125.
Therefore total cost for 850 patients = $17,625 ($15,500 + $2,125).

7   The correct answer is:

W	X	Y	Z
SV	F	V	SV

You need to adopt the high low method for each cost type to understand whether the cost is variable, semi-variable or fixed.

W:

Units	Cost
	$
100	8,000
400	10,560
40	2,560

$2,560/40 = $64 per unit; $8,000 − (100 × $64) $6,400 = $1,600 fixed cost.

140 × $64 = $8,960 + $1,600 = $10,560, therefore semi-variable so the correct answer option is either the second or fourth option.

Y:

Units	Cost
	$
100	6,500
140	9,100
40	2,600

$2,600/40 = $65 per unit; $6,500 − (100 × $65) $6,500 = $0 fixed cost, therefore it is a variable cost and the answer is the second option.

Hint. The reason we chose to calculate Y after W is that the answer could only have been the second or fourth option, and you should have noticed with product X and Z that the answers were the same for both.

8   The correct answer is: $65,800

	Units	$
High sales	34,000	73,000
Low sales	22,000	58,600
Variable cost of	12,000	14,400

Variable cost per unit $14,400/12,000 = $1.20

Fixed cost = $73,000 − (34,000 × $1.20)
        = $32,200

Estimated distribution costs for a sales volume of 28,000 units:

	$
Fixed cost	32,200
Variable cost (28,000 × $1.20)	33,600
	65,800

The first and second options are the fixed cost and variable cost respectively, rather than the total cost. If you selected the fourth option you simply calculated an average unit cost rate without allowing for the constant nature of the fixed costs.

9   The correct answer is: 30

Fixed costs = 200
Variable costs per unit = 30

10   The correct answer is: 44.5

Average x = 60/10 = 6
Average y = 1,048/10 = 104.8
       $a = \bar{y} - b\bar{x}$
       $a = 104.8 - (10.05 \times 6)$
         $= 44.5$

11   The correct answer is: 0.71

$$b = \frac{n\Sigma xy - \Sigma x\Sigma y}{n\Sigma x - (\Sigma x)^2}$$

$$b = \frac{(5 \times 83) - (45 \times 9)}{(5 \times 19) - 9^2} = \frac{10}{14} = 0.71$$

Note. $a = \Sigma y/n - b\Sigma x/n = \frac{45}{5} - \left(0.71 \times \frac{9}{5}\right) = 7.7222$

12   The correct answer is: 17,600

Output units	Total costs
350	49,100
(160)	(32,000)
190	17,100

Variable cost per unit = 17,100/190 = 90

Total cost = FC + (VC per unit × output)

49,100 = FC + (90 × 350)

FC = 17,600

13   The correct answer is: Graph 2

Graph 2 shows that costs increase in line with activity levels.

14   The correct answer is: Graph 1

Graph 1 shows that cost per unit remains the same at different levels of activity. If you chose Graph 2 then you didn't take into account that the vertical axis represented cost **per unit** in this question.

15   The correct answer is: Graph 3

Graph 3 shows that the stepped fixed costs go up in 'steps' as the level of activity increases.

16   The correct answer is: 0.63

$$r = \frac{n\sum XY - \sum X \sum Y}{\sqrt{\left(n\sum X^2 - \left(\sum X\right)^2\right)\left(n\sum Y^2 - \left(\sum Y\right)^2\right)}}$$

$$= \frac{(11 \times 13,467) - (440 \times 330)}{\sqrt{\left((11 \times 17,986) - (440)^2\right)\left((11 \times 10,366) - \left(330^2\right)\right)}}$$

$$= \frac{2,937}{\sqrt{(4,246 \times 5,126)}} = 0.63$$

17   The correct answer is: There is a very strong relationship between x and y

The correlation coefficient of 0.9 is very close to 1 and so there is a very strong relationship between x and y.

18   The correct answer is: 0.64

The correlation coefficient of determination is calculated by squaring the correlation coefficient.

4 Absorption costing

1   The correct answer is: Common costs are shared among cost centres

Costs are controlled using budgets and other management information, therefore the first option is not correct. The second option describes overhead cost absorption and the third option describes cost allocation.

2   The correct answer is: $10,160

Number of employees in packing department = 2 direct + 1 indirect = 3

Number of employees in all production departments = 15 direct + 6 indirect = 21

Packing department overhead

Canteen cost apportioned to packing department

$$= \frac{\$8,400}{21} \times 3$$
$$= \$1,200$$

Original overhead allocated and apportioned   = $8,960

Total overhead after apportionment of canteen costs   = $10,160

If you selected the first option you forgot to include the original overhead allocated and apportioned to the packing department. If you selected the second option you included the four canteen employees in your calculation, but the question states that the basis for apportionment is the number of employees in each production cost centre.

If you selected the third option you based your calculations on the direct employees only.

3   The correct answer is: Under absorbed by $2,152

Budgeted overhead absorption rate $= \dfrac{\$258,750}{11,250} = \$23$ per machine hour

	$
Overhead absorbed = $23 × 10,980 hours	252,540
Overhead incurred	254,692
Under-absorbed overhead	2,152

If you selected the second or third options you calculated the difference between the budgeted and actual overheads and interpreted the result as an under or over absorption.

If you selected the fourth option your calculations were correct but you misinterpreted the result as over absorbed.

4   The correct answer is: $25

	$
Actual overheads incurred	496,500
Over-absorbed overhead	64,375
Actual overheads absorbed	560,875

$\dfrac{\text{Actual overheads absorbed}}{\text{Actual machine hours}}$ = Amount absorbed per machine hour

$\dfrac{\$560,875}{22,435} = \$25$ per machine hour

5   The correct answer is: The service departments carry out work for each other.

There are several ways of reapportioning service department overheads to production departments. The repeated distribution method recognises inter-service department work.

6   The correct answer is: $41,972 under absorbed

Budgeted machine hours	10,960
Actual machine hours	(10,493)
Variance	467

Budgeted overheads $493,200/budgeted machine hours of 10,960 = $45 per budgeted machine hr.

$467 \times \$45 = \$21,015$

Budgeted overheads	$493,200
Actual overheads	$514,157
Variance	$20,957

Total under-absorption = $21,015 + $20,957 = $41,972.

An alternative calculation is to compare actual to absorbed overheads as follows:

OAR = $45 per machine hour (as above)

Actual overhead incurred =	$514,157
Absorbed overhead = $45 × 10,493 =	($472,185)
Difference =	$41,972 under absorbed

7   The correct answer is: 1, 2, 3 or 4

All of the overhead absorption methods are suitable, depending on the circumstances.

Method 1, direct labour hours, is suitable in a labour-intensive environment.

Method 2, machine hours, is suitable in a machine-intensive environment.

Method 3, a percentage of prime cost, can be used if it is difficult to obtain the necessary information to use a time-based method.

Method 4, a rate per unit, is suitable if all cost units are identical.

8   The correct answer is: $5.40

	$
Actual overheads	516,000
Over-absorbed overheads	24,000
Overheads absorbed by 100,000 hours	540,000

Overhead absorption rate = $540,000/100,000 = $5.40 per labour hour

The first option is incorrect because it is based on the budgeted overhead and the actual labour hours.

If you selected the second option you deducted the over-absorbed overheads by mistake, at the beginning of the calculation. If overhead is over absorbed, then the overhead absorbed must be higher than the actual overhead incurred.

The third option is incorrect because it is the actual overhead per direct labour hour.

9    $116,800

	Production centre H $	Production centre J $	Stores $	Canteen $
Overhead costs			160,000	80,000
First stores apportionment	56,000	56,000	(160,000)	48,000
			0	128,000
First canteen apportionment	64,000	57,600	6,400	(128,000)
			6,400	0
Second stores apportionment	2,240	2,240	(6,400)	1,920
			0	1,920
Second canteen apportionment	960	864	96	(1,920)
			96	0
Third stores apportionment	34	34	(96)	28
			0	28
Third canteen apportionment (approx)	14	14		(28)
	123,248	116,752		
To the nearest hundred	123,200	116,800		

10   The correct answer is: Statements 1 and 2 are true. Statement 3 is false.

Statement 1 is correct because a constant unit absorption rate is used throughout the period.

Statement 2 is correct because 'actual' overhead costs, based on actual overhead expenditure and actual activity for the period, cannot be determined until after the end of the period.

Statement 3 is incorrect because under/over absorption of overheads is caused by the use of predetermined overhead absorption rates.

11   The correct answer is: Overhead was $25,000 under-absorbed

Budget hrs	100,000	
Standard hrs	110,000	
Difference	10,000	× $2.50 = $25,000

12   The correct answer is: The value of the machinery in each cost centre

The insurance cost is likely to be linked to the cost of replacing the machines, therefore the most appropriate basis for apportionment is the value of machinery.

The other options would all be possible apportionment bases in the absence of better information, but the third option is preferable.

13   The correct answer is: $0.60 per machine hour

Department 1 appears to undertake primarily machine-based work, therefore a machine-hour rate would be most appropriate.

$$\frac{\$27,000}{45,000} = \$0.60 \text{ per machine hour}$$

The first option is not the most appropriate because it is not time-based, and most items of overhead expenditure tend to increase with time.

The second and third options are not the most appropriate because labour activity is relatively insignificant in department 1, compared with machine activity.

14   The correct answer is: $0.72 per direct labour hour

Department 2 appears to be labour-intensive therefore a direct labour-hour rate would be most appropriate.

$$\frac{\$18,000}{25,000} = \$0.72 \text{ per direct labour hour}$$

The second option is based on labour; therefore it could be suitable. However differential wage rates exist and this could lead to inequitable overhead absorption. The fourth option is not suitable because machine activity is not significant in department 2.

15   The correct answer is: $30,000

	$
Actual fixed production overheads	X
Absorbed fixed production overheads (4,500 × $8)	36,000
	6,000

Actual fixed production overheads = $36,000 − $6,000
= **$30,000**

16      $1,581,400

Depreciation should be apportioned on the basis of net book value.

Silicon moulding: $2,010,000 × (3,600/8,000) = $904,500

Power for production machinery should be apportioned on the basis of power usage.

Silicon moulding: $1,787,500 × (1,145/3,575) = $572,500

Rent and rates should be apportioned on the basis of floor space.

Silicon moulding: $261,000 × (8,000/20,000) = $104,400

Total = $904,500 + $572,500 + $104,400 = $1,581,400

---

5 Marginal costing and pricing decisions

1   The correct answer is: $23,900

	Litres
Opening inventory	(8,500)
Closing inventory	6,750
Change in inventory	(1,750)
× overhead full rate	$2
Profit difference	$3,500

Since inventories reduced during the period the absorption costing profit would be lower than the marginal costing profit. Absorption costing profit = $27,400 − $3,500 = $23,900.

2   The correct answer is: $62,300

Statement of profit or loss for period 1 under marginal costing

		Period 1	
		$	$
Sales:	Alpha (2,300 × $90)		207,000
	Beta (1,600 × $75)		120,000
			327,000
Opening inventory	Alpha	0	
	Beta	0	
Variable costs:	Alpha (2,500 × $45)	112,500	
	Beta (1,750 × $32)	56,000	
		168,500	
Less:			
Closing inventory	Alpha (200 × $45)	(9,000)	
	Beta (150 × $32)	(4,800)	
Variable cost of goods sold			154,700
Contribution			172,300
Fixed costs			(110,000)
Profit			62,300

An alternative (and quicker) calculation of marginal costing profit is as follows:

Sales units × unit contribution:

Alpha 2,300 × $45 =	$103,500
Beta 1,600 × $43 =	$68,800
Total contribution	$172,300
Less fixed overheads	($110,000)
Profit	$62,300

3   The correct answer is: $298.60

	Cost centre A	Cost centre B	Cost centre C
	$ per unit	$ per unit	$ per unit
Direct material	60.00	30.30	90.30
Direct labour	60.00	15.20	75.20
Production overhead	36.72	14.94	51.66
Total production cost			217.16
General overhead cost at 10%			21.72
Total cost			238.88
Profit margin (× 20/80)			59.72
Required selling price per unit			298.60

4   The correct answer is: $45,160

Contribution per unit	= $15 − $(4.20 + 3.00 + 1.00)
	= $6.80
Contribution for month	= $6.80 × 11,200 units
	= $76,160
Less fixed costs incurred	= $31,000
Marginal costing profit	= $45,160

The first option bases the profit on the actual sales volume at $4 per unit profit. This utilises a unit rate for fixed overhead which is not valid under marginal costing.

If you selected the third option you used the correct method but you based your calculations on the units produced rather than the units sold. If you selected the fourth option you calculated the correct contribution but you forgot to deduct the fixed overhead.

5   The correct answer is: $3,600 higher

Difference in profit = change in inventory level × fixed overhead per unit
$$= (2,400 - 2,700) \times (\$4 \times 3)$$
$$= \$3,600$$

The absorption profit will be higher because inventories have increased, and fixed overheads have been carried forward in inventories.

6   The correct answer is: 12,500

Any difference between marginal and absorption costing profit is due to changes in inventory.

	$
Absorption costing profit	2,000
Marginal costing loss	(3,000)
Difference	5,000

Change in inventory = Difference in profit/fixed product cost per unit
$$= \$5,000/\$2 = 2,500 \text{ units}$$

Marginal costing loss is lower than absorption costing profit therefore inventory has gone up – that is, production was greater than sales by 2,500 units.

Production = 10,000 units (sales) + 2,500 units = 12,500 units

7   The correct answer is: 17.55

Full cost per unit = variable cost + fixed cost
Variable cost = $10 per unit
Fixed cost = $150,000/50,000 = $3 per unit
Full cost per unit = $(10 + 3)= $13
Selling price using full cost-plus pricing method = $13 × 135% = $17.55

8   The correct answer is: $28.94

The charge for each hour of writing (to the nearest cent) should be $28.94.

Weeks worked per year   = 52 – 4 = 48
Hours worked per year   = 48 × 40 hrs
                         = 1,920

Hours chargeable to clients = 1,920 × 90% = 1,728

Total expenses = $10,000 + $40,000 = $50,000

Hourly rate = $\dfrac{\$50,000}{1,728}$ = $28.94 per hour

9   The correct answer is: $3,750,000

$ Contribution per unit   = Selling price – variable cost
                            = $25 – $15 = $10 per unit

Total contribution   = 625,000 × $10 = $6,250,000

Total fixed cost   = 500,000 × $5 = $2,500,000

Marginal costing profit   = Total contribution – total fixed costs
                            = $6,250,000 – $2,500,000
                            = $3,750,000

10   The correct answer is: $2,400 lower

Difference in profit   = Change in inventory level × fixed overhead per unit
                            = (2,500 – 2,100) × $6 = $2,400

Absorption profit is lower because the number of inventory units has decreased.

11   The correct answer is: $25,000

Increase in inventory   = (18,000 – 16,500) units
                            = 1,500 units
∴ Difference in profit   = 1,500 units × $10
                            = $15,000

Profits under marginal costing will be $15,000 less than profits under absorption costing ie $40,000 – $15,000 = $25,000.

12   $196.96

	$ per unit
Material	15.00
Labour	52.05
Production overhead (7 hrs × $9.44)	66.08
Total production cost	133.13
General overhead (8% × $133.13)	10.65
Total cost	143.78
Required return from product R	
per unit ($3,620,000 × 0.14)/9,530	53.18
Required selling price	196.96

13   The correct answer is: $45,400

		$	$
Sales	(5,200 × $30)	34,800	156,000
Direct materials	(5,800 × $6)		
Direct labour	(5,800 × $7.50)	43,500	
Variable overhead	(5,800 × $2.50)	14,500	
		92,800	
Less closing inventory	(600 × $16)	9,600	
			(83,200)
Contribution			72,800
Less fixed costs			27,400
			45,400

Or: Contribution: 5,200 × ($30 – $6 – $7.50 – $2.50) = $72,800 – $27,400 = $45,400

14   The correct answer is: $48,400

		$	$
Sales	(5,800 × $30)		156,000
Materials	(5,800 × $6)	34,800	
Labour	(5,800 × $7.50)	43,500	
Variable overhead	(5,800 × $2.50)	14,500	
Fixed costs	(5,800 × $5)	29,000	
Less closing inventory	(600 × $21)	(12,600)	
			(109,200)
Over-absorbed overhead (W)			1,600
Absorption costing profit			48,400

Workings

Overhead absorbed	(5,800 × $5)	29,000
Overhead incurred		27,400
Over-absorbed overhead		1,600

15   The correct answer is: Profit under absorption costing was higher than under marginal costing by $1,000.

Opening inventory at the beginning of July = closing inventory in June, ie 600 units. Closing inventory at the end of July is higher than opening inventory which means that absorption costing will report a higher profit than marginal costing.

Difference in profit = OAR × difference in inventory units
= $5 × 200 units
= $1,000

16   The correct answer is: $58

Marginal cost per batch = variable costs only = (3 kg × $1.20) + (2 hrs × $15) + (1 hr × $7) = $40.60
Margin is a percentage of sales.
Margin of 30% = $40.60 /0.7 = $58.00.

6 Breakeven analysis

1   The correct answer is: 2,000

Breakeven point	$= \dfrac{\$48,000}{0.4}$	= $120,000 sales value
Margin of safety (in $)	= $140,000 – $120,000	= $20,000 sales value
Margin of safety (in units)	= $20,000/$10	= 2,000 units

The second option is the breakeven point and the third option is the actual sales in units. If you selected the fourth option you calculated the margin of safety correctly as 20,000 but you misinterpreted the result as the sales volume instead of the sales value.

2   The correct answer is: Distance C

Above the breakeven point, contribution = fixed costs + profit, therefore distance C indicates the contribution at level of activity L.

Distance A indicates the profit at level of activity L, B indicates the fixed costs and D indicates the margin of safety.

3   The correct answer is: 11,886 units

New selling price ($6 × 1.1)   = $6.60
New variable cost ($1.20 × 1.1) + $0.40   = $1.72
Revised contribution per unit = $6.60 − $1.72   = $4.88
New fixed costs ($40,000 × 1.25) + $8,000   = $58,000
Revised breakeven point   = $58,000/$4.88
                                                              = 11,886 units

If you selected 8,788 units you divided the fixed cost by the selling price, but the selling price also has to cover the variable cost. 11,600 units fails to allow for the increase in variable production cost and 12,397 units increases all of the costs by the percentages given, rather than the production costs only.

4   The correct answer is: 75%

Breakeven point   = $1.10 × 4,000/$4.40
                        = 1,000 units

Margin of safety   = 4,000 − 1,000
                        = 3,000

Margin of safety ratio = 3,000/4,000 × 100%
                        = 75% of budget

5   The correct answer is: 50%

The profit/volume ratio (P/V ratio) is another term used to describe the contribution/sales ratio (C/S ratio)

$$\text{P/V ratio} = \frac{\text{Contribution per unit}}{\text{Selling price per unit}}$$

$$= \frac{\$(40 - 8 - 6 - 4 - 2)}{\$40} \times 100\% = 50\%$$

6   The correct answer is: $125,000

Breakeven point in units   = Fixed costs/contribution per unit
                                                   = $50,000/($25 × 0.4)
                                                   = 5,000

Breakeven sales revenue   = 5,000 × $25
                                                   = $125,000

Alternatively, sales revenue at breakeven point   = Fixed costs/CS ratio
                                                   = $50,000/0.4
                                                   = $125,000

7   The correct answer is: 8,000

The third option gives the breakeven point in terms of sales value:

$$\frac{\$80,000}{0.2} = \$400,000$$

To convert this to a number of units we would need to divide by the selling price per unit.
$400,000/$50 = 8,000

8 The correct answers are: Changes in inventory levels are ignored. A change in the selling price per unit will alter the slope of the line on a P/V chart. An assumption is made that variable costs per unit are the same at all levels of output.

CVP analysis assumes that sales = production (ie that there is no change in inventory levels) and that variable costs per unit are the same over the relevant range.

However, a change in the estimate of those variable costs per unit over the whole range will change the slope of the line on a P/V chart. A change in the estimate of fixed costs will not alter the slope of the line, but will change the point of intersection with the vertical axis. It is possible to analyse more than one product using a breakeven chart, but only if the sales mix is the same over the relevant range.

9 The correct answer is: 4,300 units

Sales units that will earn a required profit = (fixed costs + required profit)/unit contribution
= ($12,518 + $8,982)/$5
= 4,300

10 The correct answer is: 9,000

We can determine the **value** of breakeven sales as $90,000/0.4 = $225,000, but this does not tell us the number of units required to break even. $225,000/$25 = 9,000

11 The correct answer is: 90,000

	$
Total cost of 150,000 units ($\times$ $41.50)	6,225,000
Total cost of 100,000 units ($\times$ $47.50)	4,750,000
Variable cost of 50,000 units	1,475,000
Variable cost per unit	$29.50

Substituting:	$
Total cost of 100,000 units	4,750,000
Variable cost of 100,000 units ($\times$ $29.50)	2,950,000
Fixed costs	1,800,000

$$\therefore \text{ Breakeven point} = \frac{\$1,800,000}{\$(49.50 - 29.50)} = 90,000 \text{ units}$$

If you selected the first option you divided the fixed cost by the unit selling price, but the variable costs must also be taken into account. If you selected the third option you assumed that the production overheads and the marketing and administration costs were wholly fixed. In fact the marketing costs are the only wholly fixed costs. You can test this by multiplying the unit rate by the output volume at each level of activity. If you selected the fourth option you divided the fixed cost by the profit per unit instead of the contribution per unit.

12 The correct answer is: Distance C

Contribution at level of activity x = sales value less variable costs, which is indicated by distance C. Distance A indicates the profit at activity x, B indicates the fixed costs and D indicates the margin of safety in terms of sales value.

13   The correct answer is: $5.60

Workings

Sales are 60,000 units at the normal level of activity. Variable costs at 60,000 units of production/sales are as follows.

	$	$ per unit
Production overhead	30,000	0.50
Sales costs (5% of $600,000)	30,000	0.50
Distribution costs	15,000	0.25
Administration overhead	9,000	0.15
	84,000	1.40
Direct costs	180,000	3.00
Total variable costs	264,000	4.40
Sales revenue	600,000	10.00
Contribution	336,000	5.60

14   The correct answer is: $252,000.

	$
Fixed costs	
Production overhead	126,000
Sales costs	50,000
Distribution costs	45,000
Administration overhead	31,000
	252,000

15   The correct answer is: 45,000

$$\text{Breakeven point} = \frac{\text{Fixed costs}}{\text{Contribution per unit}}$$

$$= \frac{\$252,000}{\$5.60}$$

$$= 45,000 \text{ units}$$

16   The correct answer is: $275,000

Breakeven sales revenue = Fixed costs / Contribution to sales ratio
Fixed costs per month = production cost of $90,000 + selling costs of $20,000 ($240,000/12) = $110,000
Breakeven sales revenue = $110,000 / (80,000/200,000)
Breakeven sales revenue = $275,000

7 Limiting factor analysis

1   First product: K
    Second product: L
    Third product: J

	Product J	Product K	Product L
	$ per unit	$ per unit	$ per unit
Selling price	140	122	134
Variable cost	106	86	77
Contribution	34	36	57
Kg of material	11	7	13
Contribution per kg	$3.09	$5.14	$4.39
Ranking	3	1	2

2   The correct answer is: Product B most profitable, Product C least profitable

	Product A	Product B	Product C
Contribution per unit	$205.00	$270.00	$250.00
Kg required per unit	10	5	15
Contribution per kg of material	$20.50	$54.00	$16.67
Ranking	2	1	3

3   The correct answer is: Material only

	Quantity per unit	Quantity required	Quantity available
Material ($72 ÷ $8)	9 litres (× 2,000)	18,000 litres	16,000 litres
Labour ($49 ÷ $7)	7 hours (× 2,000)	14,000 hours	15,000 hours

4   The correct answer is: 10,000

Workings

	Product T1	Product T2	Product T3	Total
Machine hours required per unit	5	3	6	
Maximum demand (units)	9,000	8,000	11,000	
Total machine hours required	45,000	24,000	66,000	135,000
Machine hours available				125,000
Deficiency in machine hours for next period				10,000

5   The correct answer is: FEEB should manufacture 10,000 units of FE and 5,000 units of EB.

	FE	EB
	$ per unit	$ per unit
Variable cost of making	15	21
Variable cost of buying	24	27
Extra variable cost of buying	9	6
Raw material saved by buying	1.5 kg	2 kg
Extra variable cost of buying per kg saved	$6	$3
	1st	2nd

Production plan

	Kg
Make FE (10,000 × 1.5 kg)	15,000
EB (5,000 × 2 kg)	10,000
Total materials consumed (maximum available)	25,000

The remaining 2,000 units of EB should be purchased from the subcontractor.

6   The correct answer is: Product M most profitable, Product K least profitable

	Product K	Product L	Product M
Contribution per unit	$57	$83	$79
Labour hours per unit	3	4	3
Contribution per labour hour	$19	$20.75	$26.33
Ranking	3	2	1

Therefore M is the most profitable and K is the least profitable.

If you selected the first option you reversed the ranking. The second option ranks the products according to the contribution per unit, but this takes no account of the limiting factor. If you selected the fourth option you ranked the products according to their profit per unit, but this takes no account of the limiting factor and is distorted by the fixed costs.

7   The correct answer is: B A T

This answer ranks the products by contribution per kg of material (the limiting factor).

	B	A	T	Total
Maximum sales units	1,000	1,200	1,500	
Material kg needed	1,000	2,400	4,500	7,900
Labour hours needed	2,000	2,400	4,500	8,900

Thus, labour is not a limiting factor but material is a limiting factor.

Rank the products by contribution per kg of material.

	B	A	T
Contribution per unit ($)	50	60	55
Kg of material per unit	1	2	3
Contribution per kg of material ($)	50	30	18.3
Rank by contribution per kg of material	1	2	3

8   The correct answer is: $600,000

To maximise contribution, we must produce the product with the greatest contribution per $ spent on labour.

	X	Y	Z
	$ per unit	$ per unit	$ per unit
Contribution per unit	50	40	60
Labour cost per unit	30	10	5
Contribution per $ of labour	1.67	4	12
Ranking	3	2	1

Thus the company will make $50,000/5 = 10,000 units of Z.

This will produce 10,000 × $60 = $600,000 of contribution.

9   The correct answers are: Fixed costs in total are not changed by changes in production. Variable costs per unit are not changed by changes in production. Sales demand, prices and resources required for each product are known with certainty.

Fixed costs in total are not changed by changes in production (so that the profit-maximising and contribution-maximising output levels are the same). Variable costs per unit are not changed by changes in production and sales demand, prices and resources required for each product are known with certainty (so that contribution per unit of scarce resource is constant).

10 The correct answer is: $43,315

Calculate production plan

Material available	5,000 kg
Maximum sales of B (1,000 units × 1 kg)	(1,000 kg)
Maximum sales of A (1,200 units × 2 kg)	(2,400 kg)
Produce as many units as possible of T = 533 units	(1,600 kg)

Calculate contribution

	B	A	T	Total
Units made and sold	1,000	1,200	533	
Contribution ($)	50,000	72,000	29,315	151,315

Profit = Budgeted contribution – fixed overheads

Remember, changing the production plan will not alter the total fixed costs, which must therefore be calculated from budgeted (not actual) production.

Fixed costs = (1,000 × $30) + (1,200 × $40) + (1,500 × $20) = $(30,000 + 48,000 + 30,000) = $108,000

Maximum profit = $151,315 – $108,000 = $43,315

11 The correct answer is: Component Y only

	Product X	Product Y	Product Z
	$ per unit	$ per unit	$ per unit
Subcontractor price	8	14	11
Variable cost	5	16	10
Difference	3	–2	1

12 The correct answer is: 1st = V1, 2nd = V3, 3rd = V2

	V1	V2	V3
	$	$	$
Selling price per unit	30	36	34.00
Variable cost per unit	14	22	25.40
Contribution per unit	16	14	8.60
Labour cost per unit	$4	$8	$3.60
Contribution per $ of labour cost	$4	$1.75	$2.39
Rank order of production	1	2	3

13   The correct answer is: 13,000 hours

Workings

	Product A	Product B	Product C	Total
Machine hours required per unit	6	4	7	
Maximum demand (units)	3,000	2,500	5,000	
Total machine hours required	18,000	10,000	35,000	63,000
Machine hours available				50,000
Deficiency in machine hours for next period				13,000

14   The correct answers are:

Contribution per machine hour (Product A) = $7.67
Contribution per machine hour (Product B) = $11.50
Contribution per machine hour (Product C) = $6.57

Workings

	Product A	Product B	Product C
	$	$	$
Selling price per unit	200	158	224
Variable cost per unit	154	112	178
Contribution per unit	46	46	46
Machine hours per unit	6	4	7
Contribution per machine hour	$7.67	$11.50	$6.57

15   The correct answer is: $115,000

2,500 × $46 = $115,000

16   The correct answer is: Product Ting

In a make or buy situation without limiting factors, the cost of purchasing from an external supplier is compared to the relevant cost of production (all variable costs plus directly attributable fixed costs).

	Spring	Ping	Ting
	$	$	$
Direct material	6	9	7
Direct labour	15	12	15
Directly attributable fixed costs	5	2	3
Relevant cost of production	26	23	25
Cost of purchasing from supplier	27	24	23
Difference	-1	-1	2

8 Standard costing

1   The correct answer is: A standard that can be attained if production is carried out efficiently, machines are operated properly and/or materials are used properly. Some allowance is made for waste and inefficiencies.

Attainable standards may provide an incentive for employees to work harder as they represent a realistic but challenging target of efficiency.

A standard which is based on currently attainable working conditions describes a current standard. Current standards do not attempt to improve current levels of efficiency.

A standard which is established for use over a long period and which is used to show trends describes a basic standard. Basic standards are not particularly useful for control nor for motivating employees.

A standard which can be attained under perfect operating conditions, and which does not include an allowance for wastage, spoilage, machine breakdowns and other inefficiencies describes an ideal standard. Ideal standards are not very useful for day-to-day control and they can demotivate employees because they are highly unlikely to be achieved.

2   The correct answer is: $38

Overhead absorption rate	= $37,500/2,500
	= $15 per unit
Direct cost	= $23 per unit
Standard total production cost	= $15 + $23
	= $38 per unit

3   The correct answer is: $89.50

Direct material X (15 × $3)	$45.00
Direct material Y (8 × $4)	$32.00
Direct labour (2 × $6.25)	$12.50
Standard cost per frying pan	$89.50

4   The correct answer is: $90

		$ per unit	$ per unit
Material P	7 kg × $4	28	
Material S	3 kg × $9	27	
			55
Direct labour	5 hr × $7		35
Standard prime cost of product J			90

The first option is the standard material cost and the third option is the standard total production cost, including overheads which are not part of prime cost.

The fourth option includes the absorption of general overhead; always **read the question carefully**!

5   The correct answer is: $31,500

Hours taken per aeroplane = 1,500/1,200
                           = 1.25 hours per aeroplane
Time saving   = 1,200 × (1.5 hours − 1.25 hours)
                           = 300 hours
Basic wage   = 1,500 hours × $20
                           = $30,000
Bonus paid   = 300 hours × 25% × $20
                           = $1,500
Total earnings   = $31,500

6   The correct answer is: 520

	Units produced		Standard hours per unit		Standard hours produced
Sheds	270	×	1.2	=	324
Tables	80	×	0.7	=	56
Workbenches	140	×	1.0	=	140
					520

The first option is the total number of units produced, but there is very little meaning in adding together such **dissimilar units**. The second option is the actual hours worked, which is **not a measure of output**. If you selected the fourth option you multiplied the total units by the combined time for one unit of each product. This would only be applicable if the products were manufactured in **batches**, and then we would have to express the output in terms of batches, rather than in terms of total units produced.

7   The correct answer is: The amount of work achievable in an hour, when working at standard efficiency levels

A standard hour is the quantity of output achievable, at standard performance, in an hour. It is often used to measure total output when **dissimilar units** are made.

The situation described in the first option is **ideal operating conditions**, and the second option describes a typical situation for many organisations that are involved in mass production.

8   The correct answer is: A standard that is kept unchanged, to show the trend in costs

A basic standard is established for use over a long period and is used to show trends. The other options describe ideal, attainable, and current standards respectively.

9   The correct answer is: The operating standards set for production should be the attainable level.

It is generally accepted that the use of **attainable standards** has the optimum motivational impact on employees. Some allowance is made for unavoidable wastage and inefficiencies, but the attainable level can be reached if production is carried out efficiently.

10   The correct answer is: 1.25 litres

Required liquid input = 1 litre × $\frac{100}{80}$ = 1.25 litres

11 The correct answer is: Focusing management reports on areas that require attention and ignoring those that appear to be performing within acceptable limits

When management by exception is operated within a standard costing system, only the variances which exceed acceptable tolerance limits need to be investigated by management with a view to control action. Adverse and favourable variances alike may be subject to investigation, therefore the first option is incorrect.

Any efficient information system would ensure that only managers who are able to act on the information receive management reports, even if they are not prepared on the basis of management by exception. Therefore the second option is incorrect.

12 The correct answer is: 1, 2 and 3 only

Standard costing provides targets for achievement, and yardsticks against which actual performance can be monitored (**item 1**). It also provides the unit cost information for evaluating the volume figures contained in a budget (**item 2**). Inventory control systems are simplified with standard costing. Once the variances have been eliminated, all inventory units are valued at standard price (**item 3**).

Item 4 is incorrect because standard costs are an estimate of what will happen in the future, and a unit cost target that the organisation is aiming to achieve.

13 The correct answer is: Ideal

Staff are responsible for meeting the standard so an ideal standard which is almost impossible to meet, will have a demotivational effect on staff.

14 The correct answer is: $90.00

Standard labour cost per unit = 9 hours $\times \dfrac{100}{90} \times \$9 = \$90$

15 The correct answer is: False

They may be used in a marginal costing system as well.

9 Flexible budgeting

1 The correct answer is: $4,755 Adverse

The volume variance is the increase in cost resulting from a change in the volume of activity, ie the difference between the original budget and the flexed budget.

Volume variance = $126,100 − $130,855
               = $4,755 (A)

2 The correct answer is: A budget that, by recognising different cost behaviour patterns, is designed to change as the volume of activity changes

A flexible budget can help managers to make more valid comparisons. It is designed to show the allowed expenditure for the actual number of units produced and sold. By comparing this flexible budget with the actual expenditure, it is possible to distinguish genuine efficiencies.

3   The correct answer is:

Budget	Actual
$	$
33,180	29,666

The budget and actual figures in the question are not comparable as the volumes are different (700 vs 790 units) and thus the revenues/costs will vary due to the different output. The original budget needs to be flexed to actual volumes of 790 units as given below:

$29,400/700 units $\times$ 790 units = $33,180.

The flexed budget of $33,180 is now comparable with the actual figure of $29,666 leading to a variance of $3,514 ($33,180 – $29,666).

4   The correct answer is: $115,000

Activity	Overhead
	$
50%	100,000
75%	112,500
25%	12,500

$ 12,500/25 = $500 increase as activity increases by 1%

Therefore an increase of 5% activity would be $112,500 + (500 $\times$ 5) $2,500 = $115,000.

5    $37,800

	Units	$
High activity	3,000	32,600
Low activity	2,000	27,400
Increase	1,000	5,200

Variable cost per unit $= \dfrac{\$5,200}{1,000} = \$5.20$ per unit

Fixed cost, substituting in high activity $= \$32,600 - (3,000 \times \$5.20)$
$= \$17,000$

Budget cost allowance for 4,000 units:	$
Variable cost (4,000 $\times$ $5.20)	20,800
Fixed cost	17,000
	37,800

6   The correct answer is: 8,688

Direct material cost per 1% = $30

Direct labour and production overhead:

			$
At	90%	activity	6,240
At	80%	activity	6,180
Change	10%		60

Variable cost per 1% activity = $60/10% = $6

Substituting in 80% activity:

Fixed cost of labour and production overhead $= \$6,180 - (80 \times \$6)$
$= \$5,700$

Flexed budget cost allowance:

	$
Direct material $30 × 83	2,490
Direct labour and production overhead:	
variable $6 × 83	498
fixed	5,700
	8,688

7   The correct answer is: $2,725 Adverse

The expenditure variance is the difference between the flexed budget and the actual results.

Expenditure variance   = $130,855 – $133,580
                         = $2,725 (A)

8   The correct answer is: $14,700

	Units	$
High activity	3,000	12,900
Low activity	2,000	11,100
Increase	1,000	1,800

Variable cost per unit $= \dfrac{\$1,800}{1,000} = \$1.80$ per unit

Fixed cost, substituting in high activity   = $12,900 – (3,000 × $1.80)
                                            = $7,500

	$
Budget cost allowance for 4,000 units:	
Variable cost (4,000 × $1.80)	7,200
Fixed cost	7,500
	14,700

The first option is the variable cost allowance only and the second option is the fixed cost allowance only. If you selected the third option your variable cost per unit calculation was upside down ($1,000/1,800 instead of $1,800/1,000).

9   The correct answer is: $41,000

Contribution for 10,000 units

	$'000
Sales revenue	150
Direct material	(45)
Direct labour	(30)
Variable overhead	(20)
	55

	$
∴ contribution for 12,000 units = 55 × 1.2 =	66,000
Less fixed costs	25,000
Flexed budget profit for 12,000 units	41,000

If you selected the first option you flexed the allowance for variable costs correctly but you did not flex the budgeted sales revenue. The second option is the original budgeted profit for 10,000 units. If you selected the third option you flexed the fixed overhead cost, which is not correct; fixed overheads are not affected by changes in volume.

10   The correct answer is: $1,188,550

A 10% activity increase in 20X3 increased costs by $23,000 ($1,100,000 – $1,077,000).

As fixed costs do not change with output, any change in costs must have been the result of a change in variable costs.

If 100% of the variable costs in 20X2 were $230,000 (23,000 divided by 10%), fixed costs must have been $847,000 ($1,077,000 – $230,000). Variable costs in 20X3 were therefore, $253,000 (230,000 × 1 + 10%).

A 35% increase in 20X3 variable costs of $253,000 to $341,550 gives a total cost of $1,188,550 ($847,000 + $341,550).

11   The correct answer is: $370,300

Direct material cost per 1% activity = $2,000
Direct labour cost per 1% activity   = $1,500

Production overhead		$
At	60% activity	54,000
At	80% activity	62,000
Change	20%	8,000

Variable cost per 1% change in activity = $\dfrac{\$8,000}{20}$ = $400

Substituting in 80% activity:

	$
Variable cost = 80 × $400	32,000
Total cost	62,000
∴ Fixed cost	30,000

Other overhead is a wholly fixed cost.

Budget flexed at 77% level of activity

	$'000
Direct material 77 × $2,000	154.0
Direct labour 77 × $1,500	115.5
Production overhead:	
Variable 77 × $400	30.8
Fixed	30.0
Other overhead	40.0
	370.3

If you selected the first option you did not include a fixed cost allowance for the other overhead. The third option ignores the fact that production overhead is a semi-variable cost and the fourth option simply multiplies the total cost for 70% activity by a factor of 1.1. This makes no allowance for the fact that there is an element of fixed costs within production overhead, and other overhead is wholly fixed.

12   The correct answer is: $14,700

Variable cost per unit $= \dfrac{\$12,900 - \$11,100}{(6,000 - 4,000) \text{ units}}$

$= \dfrac{\$1,800}{2,000 \text{ units}} = \$0.90 \text{ per cent}$

Fixed costs $= \$11,100 - (4,000 \times \$0.90)$
$= \$11,100 - \$3,600 = \$7,500$

∴ Budgeted cost allowance for an activity level of 8,000 units is

	$
Fixed cost	7,500
Variable cost ($0.90 × 8,000)	7,200
	14,700

If you selected the first option you did not include an allowance for fixed cost, and if you selected the other two options you calculated the allowance on a pro rata basis from the data given. This does not take account of the fixed element of the production cost.

13   The correct answers are:

A $20,000

B $20,000

C $36,000

D $36,000

E $36,000

We are told supervision is a step cost. For 4,000 and 5,000 units the budget will be $20,000. Over 5,000 units the budget will be $20,000 + $16,000 = $36,000. Example: budget for 6,000 units = $36,000.

14   The correct answers are:

F $18,000

G $18,000

H $18,000

I $21,000

J $24,000

If the minimum charge is payable on all production up to and including 6,000 units, then it is paid on production of 4,000 units and is $18,000. This represents a fixed cost at all levels of production. On production over 6,000 units there is a variable charge based on power consumed.

Production of 8,000 units will have incurred the variable charge on 2,000 units. This variable charge for 2,000 units = $(24,000 - 18,000) = $6,000. The charge per unit = $6,000/2,000 = $3.

For production up to 6,000 units, the budget is $18,000. For production over 6,000 units, the budget is $18,000 plus $3 per unit over 6,000 units.

Example: budget for 7,000 units = $18,000 + ((7,000 - 6,000) × $3) = $21,000

15   The correct answers are:

K $12,000

L $14,000

M $16,000

N $18,000

O $20,000

A doubling of production does not result in a doubling of cost. Indirect materials is therefore a mixed cost.

Consider the total cost of 4,000 units.

	$
Variable cost (4,000 × $2)	8,000
Total cost	12,000
Fixed cost	4,000

The total cost of indirect materials is therefore based on a fixed cost of $4,000 plus a variable of $2 per unit. Example: budget for 6,000 units = $4,000 + $(6,000 × 2) = $16,000.

10 Budget preparation

1   The correct answer is: Cash budget

A functional budget is a budget prepared for a particular function or department. A cash budget is **the cash result of the planning decisions included in all the functional budgets**. It is not a functional budget itself.

The production budget, the distribution cost budget and the selling cost budget are all prepared for specific functions, therefore they are functional budgets.

2   The correct answer is: 2, 4, 5, 1, 6, 3

Since there are no production resource limitations, sales would be the principal budget factor and the sales budget (2) would be prepared first. Budgeted inventory changes included in the finished goods inventory budget (4) would then indicate the required production for the production budget (5). This would lead to the calculation of the material usage (1) which would then be adjusted for the budgeted change in material inventory (6) to determine the required level of budgeted material purchases (3).

If you selected the first option you began with production as the principal budget factor. However, there are no production resource limitations so production output is not a limiting factor. If you selected the other options you correctly identified sales as the principal budget factor, but you did not identify the correct flow through the inventory adjustments to determine the required production and material purchases.

3   The correct answer is: 175,000

Required increase in finished goods inventory   1,000
Budgeted sales of Alpha   60,000
Required production   61,000

                                                      kg
Raw materials usage budget (× 3 kg)   183,000
Budgeted decrease in raw materials inventory   (8,000)
Raw materials purchase budget   175,000

If you selected the first option you made no allowance for the increase in finished goods inventory. If you selected the third option you did not adjust for the budgeted decrease in raw materials inventory, and the fourth option adjusts for an increase in raw materials inventory, rather than a decrease.

4   The correct answer is: $49,480

                                                       $
August sales $60,000 × 60% × 98%*   35,280
July sales $40,000 × 25%   10,000
June sales $35,000 × 12%   4,200
                                                 49,480

*This reduction allows for the 2% settlement discount.

If you selected the first option you misinterpreted 'month after sale' to be the month the sale was made. The invoices are issued on the last day of each month, therefore cash receipts in respect of each month's sales will begin in the following month.

The third option makes no allowance for the settlement discount and the fourth option includes the receipt of bad debts; those amounts will never be received cash.

5   The correct answer is: 23,100

                                                  Quarter 4
                                                    Units
Total sales volume (7,750 + 8,000 + 7,500)   23,250
Required closing inventory (20% × 7,000)   1,400
                                                   24,650
Less opening inventory (20% × 7,750)   1,550
                                                   23,100

6   The correct answer is: $1,115,977

Receivables will rise by 12% so closing receivables = $163,525 × 112%
                                                     = $183,148

Cash received = Sales + opening receivables − closing receivables
               = $1,135,600 + $163,525 − $183,148
               = $1,115,977

7   The correct answer is: 51%

Cost of sales = Opening inventory + purchases – closing inventory
            = $112,250 + $751,700 – $113,500
            = $750,450

$750,450 + mark-up = $1,135,600
Mark-up = $385,150
Mark-up % = 385,150/750,450 = 51%

8   The correct answers are: Arrange an overdraft. Implement better credit control procedures.

Replace non-current assets is incorrect as replacing non-current assets cost money. Pay suppliers early is incorrect because paying suppliers early would make the situation worse. Increasing inventory would not provide any extra cash.

9   The correct answer is: $121,440

June sales $100,000 × 15% = $15,000
July sales $150,000 × 20% = $30,000
August sales $130,000 × 60% =$78,000 less 2% discount $1,560 = $76,440
Total = $15,000 + $30,000 + $76,440 = $121,440

10   The correct answer is: 367,500 kg

Product A:

Opening inventory 5,000
Closing inventory 6,500 (5000 + (5000 × 30%))

Sales required = 70,000 units therefore production of 71,500 units required (70,000 + 6,500 – 5,000)

Material X requirements:

Opening inventory   50,000 kg
Closing inventory   60,000 kg

71,500 units × 5 g = 357,500 kg

Therefore need to purchase = 367,500 kg (357,500 + 60,000 – 50,000)

11   The correct answer is: Factor that limits the activities of the organisation and is often the starting point in budget preparation

The principal budget factor can also be known as the limiting factor as this factor usually indicates which budget should be prepared first. Failure to identify the principal budgeting factor at an early stage could lead to delays at a later stage when managers realise targets that were set are not feasible.

12   The correct answers are: Funds from a bond issue. Interest on a loan

A cash budget is used by businesses to forecast cash inflows and cash outflows so as to identify potential cash shortfalls or surpluses that may require management action. Funds received from a bond issue will appear as an inflow (receipt) in the cash budget while interest on a loan will be an outflow (pay-out). A cash budget will exclude non-cash items like depreciation and bad debts written off as these are book entries with no cash impact.

BPP
LEARNING
MEDIA

13   The correct answer is: 255 units

Production budget

Production = sales + closing inventory – opening inventory

	Units	Units
Budgeted sales		280
Closing inventory	5	
Opening inventory	(30)	
Decrease in inventory		(25)
Budgeted production		255

14   The correct answer is: 1,785 kg, $89,250

Materials usage budget

Production	255 units
× usage per unit	× 7 kg
Total budgeted usage in kg	1,785 kg
× budgeted cost per kg	× $50
Total budgeted usage in $	$89,250

15   The correct answer is: $7,650

Labour utilisation budget – grade 0

Budgeted production	255 units
× hrs per unit	× 2 hrs
Total budgeted labour hrs	510 hrs
× budgeted cost per hr	× $15
Budgeted labour cost	$7,650

---

11 Variance analysis

1   The correct answer is: $328 (A)

	$
8,200 kg did cost	6,888
but should have cost (× $0.80)	6,560
	328 (A)

If you selected the first two options you based your calculations on the materials issued to production. However, the material inventory account is maintained at standard cost; therefore the material price variance is calculated when the materials are purchased. If you selected the fourth option you calculated the size of the variance correctly but you misinterpreted it as favourable.

2   The correct answer is: $152 (A)

870 units did use	7,150 kg
but should have cost (× $0.80)	6,960 kg
Usage variance in kg	190 (A)
× standard cost per kg	× $0.80
	152 (A)

If you selected the first option you calculated the size of the variance correctly but you misinterpreted it as favourable. If you selected the third option you evaluated the usage variance in kg at the actual price per kg, instead of the standard price per kg. The fourth option bases the calculation of standard usage on the budgeted production of 850 units. This is not comparing like with like.

3   The correct answer is: $2,500 (A)

	$
2,300 hours should have cost (× $7)	16,100
but did cost	18,600
Rate variance	2,500 (A)

The first option is the total direct labour cost variance. If you selected the second option you calculated the correct money value of the variance but you misinterpreted its direction. If you selected the fourth option you based your calculation on the 2,200 hours worked, but 2,300 hours were paid for and these hours should be the basis for the calculation of the rate variance.

4   The correct answer is: $2,800 (F)

260 units should have taken (× 10 hrs)	2,600 hrs
but took (active hours)	2,200 hrs
Efficiency variance in hours	400 hrs (F)
× standard rate per hour	× $7
Efficiency variance in $	$ 2,800 (F)

The first option is the total direct labour cost variance. If you selected the second option you based your calculations on the 2,300 hours paid for; but efficiency measures should be based on the **active hours only**, ie 2,200 hours.

If you selected the third option you calculated the correct money value of the variance but you misinterpreted its direction.

5   The correct answer is: $5,000 (F)

The correct labour efficiency variance is calculated as follows, comparing budgeted hours with actual hours spent for the production achieved.

((11,000 units × 0.75 hrs) − 8,000 hrs) × $20 per hr = $5,000 favourable

6   The correct answer is: $12,000 (A)

The correct variable overhead variance is calculated by comparing the budgeted variable overheads per labour hour worked with the actual variable overheads incurred during the month.

(8,000 hours × $15 per labour hour − $132,000) = $12,000 Adverse

7   The correct answers are:, $1,200 (F), $900 (A)

	$
200 units should sell for (× $70)	14,000
but did sell for	15,200
Sales price variance	1,200 (F)

BPP LEARNING MEDIA

The budgeted contribution per unit $= \dfrac{\text{budgeted monthly contribution}}{\text{budgeted monthly sales volume}}$

$$= \frac{\$6,900}{230} = \$30 \text{ per unit}$$

Budgeted sales volume	230
Actual sales volume	200
Sales volume variance in units	30
× standard contribution per unit	× $30
Sales volume contribution variance	$900 (A)

8   The correct answers are:

(a)

Variance	Favourable	Unfavourable
Material price	Unforeseen discounts received	
Material usage		Defective material
Labour rate		Wage rate increase

(b)

Variance	Favourable	Unfavourable
Labour efficiency		Lack of training of production workers
Variable overhead expenditure	More economical use of non-material resources	
Idle time		Machine breakdown

Unforeseen discounts received would reduce the actual purchase price as compared to the standard cost expected and would thus lead to a favourable material price variance.

Use of defective material is likely to increase the wastage of raw material in the production process leading to a higher than expected raw material usage. Unforeseen discounts received would reduce the actual material price and so the actual cost would be lower than the standard cost. This would therefore lead to a favourable material price variance.

Higher wage rate increases mean that labour was paid more than the budgeted rate leading to an adverse labour rate variance.

9   The correct answer is: $564,000 (F)

	$
11,750 units should have cost (× $20 × 15 kg)	3,525,000
But did cost	2,961,000
	564,000 (F)

10   The correct answer is: $258,948

Standard marginal costing reconciliation

	$
Original budgeted contribution	290,000
Sales volume variance	(36,250)
Standard contribution from actual sales	253,750
Selling price variance	21,875
	275,625
Variable cost variances	
Total direct material variance	(6,335)
Total direct labour variance	11,323
Total variable overhead variance	(21,665)
Actual contribution	258,948

11   The correct answer is: 18,700

Production should have taken	X hours
But did take	17,500 hours
Variance in hours	X – 17,500 hours (F)
× standard rate per hour	× $6.50
Variance in $	$7,800 (F)

∴ 6.5(X – 17,500) = 7,800
X – 17,500 = 1,200
X = 18,700

The first option is the efficiency variance in terms of hours, and option C is the actual hours worked.

If you selected the second option you treated the efficiency variance as adverse instead of favourable.

12   The correct answer is: 1 and 2 only

Statement 1 is consistent with an adverse material price variance. Higher quality material is likely to cost more. Statement 2 is consistent with an adverse material price variance. Removal of bulk discounts would result in a higher material price.

Statement 3 is not consistent with an adverse material price variance. **Favourable** variances would result if the standard price was set too high.

13   The correct answer is: $672 (A)

Standard variable overhead cost per unit = $3,120/520 units
= $6 per unit

	$
Standard variable overhead cost for 560 units (× $6)	3,360
Actual variable overhead cost	4,032
	672 (A)

If you selected the first option you compared the standard cost for 560 units with the standard cost for 520 units. This indicates the **volume effect** of the change in output but it is not the total variable production overhead cost variance.

If you selected the third option you calculated the correct money value of the variance but you misinterpreted its direction.

The fourth option is the difference between the standard cost for 520 units and the actual cost for 560 units. This is not a valid comparison for **control purposes** because of the **different output volumes**.

14   The correct answer is: $448 (F)

Standard variable production overhead cost per hour = $3,120/1,560

                                        = $2

	$
2,240 hours of variable production overhead should cost ($\times$ $2)	4,480
But did cost	4,032
	448 (F)

If you selected the second option you calculated the correct money value of the variance but you misinterpreted its direction. The third option is the variable production overhead total variance. If you selected the fourth option you made the same error as for the fourth option in question 1.

15   The correct answer is: $1,120 (A)

Standard time allowed for one unit = 1,560 hours/520 units

                                      = 3 hours

560 units should take ($\times$ 3 hours)	1,680 hours
But did take	2,240 hours
Efficiency variance in hours	560 hours (A)
$\times$ standard variable production overhead per hr	$\times$ $2 (from answer to Q14)
	$1,120 (A)

If you selected the first option you valued the efficiency variance in hours at the actual variable production overhead rate per hour.

If you selected the third option you calculated the correct money value of the variance but you misinterpreted its direction.

If you selected the fourth option you based your calculation on the difference between the original budgeted hours for 520 units and the actual hours worked for 560 units. This is **not comparing like with like**.

---

12 Job and batch costing

1   The correct answer is: $2,400

Active hours required	380
Add idle time (5/95)	20
Total hours to be paid	400 @ $6 per hour
Total labour cost	$2,400

If you selected the first option you reduced the active hours by 5%. However, the hours to be paid must be **greater than** the active hours, therefore the idle hours must be added. If you selected the second option you made no allowance for the idle hours, which must also be paid for. If you selected the third option you added 5% to the active hours, but note that the idle time is quoted as a **percentage of the total time to be paid for**.

2   The correct answer is: $20,800

	Dept A $	Dept B $	Total $
Direct materials	5,000	3,000	8,000
Direct labour	1,600	1,000	2,600
Production overhead	1,600	800	2,400
Absorption production cost			13,000
Other overheads (20%)			2,600
Cost of the job			15,600
Profit (25% of sales = 33% of the cost)			5,200
Sales price			20,800

If you selected the third option you calculated the profit margin as 25% of total cost, instead of 25% of selling price.

If you selected the second option you forgot to add administration overhead, and the first option contains the same error with the profit calculated incorrectly as 25% of cost.

3   The correct answer is: $606

	$
Selling price of job	1,690
Less profit margin (30/130)	390
Total cost of job	1,300
Less overhead	694
Prime cost	606

If you selected the first option you deducted 30% from the selling price to derive the total cost of the job. The third option is the result of deducting the overhead from the selling price, but omitting to deduct the profit margin. The fourth option is the total cost of the job; you needed to deduct the overhead to derive the prime cost.

4   The correct answers are: Production of the product is of a relatively short duration and Production relates to a single special order.

Job costing is appropriate where each cost unit is separately identifiable and is of relatively short duration.

5   The correct answer is: $40,800

Hours to be paid for × 90% = 4,590

∴ Hours to be paid for = 4,590 ÷ 0.9 = 5,100

Budgeted labour cost = $8 × 5,100 hr = $40,800

6   The correct answer is: Production is carried out in accordance with the wishes of the customer.

Job costing is a costing method applied where work is **undertaken to customers' special requirements**. The second option describes process costing, the third describes service costing and the fourth describes absorption costing.

7   The correct answers are: $326,000 and $2.92

$103,000 + $105,000 + $84,000 + $34,000 = $326,000

($103,000 + $105,000 + $84,000)/100,000 = $2.92

8   The correct answers are: Actual material cost. Absorbed manufacturing overheads. Actual labour cost.

The actual material and labour costs for a batch can be determined from the material and labour recording system. Actual manufacturing overheads cannot be determined for a specific batch because of the need for allocation and apportionment of each item of overhead expenditure, and the subsequent calculation of a predetermined overhead absorption rate. Therefore 'actual manufacturing overheads' is incorrect and 'absorbed manufacturing overheads' is correct.

9   The correct answer is: $124.50

Production overhead absorption rate = $240,000/30,000 = $8 per labour hour
Other overhead absorption rate = ($150,000/$750,000) × 100% = 20% of total production cost

Job B124	$
Direct materials (3 kg × $5)	15.00
Direct labour (4 hours × $9)	36.00
Production overhead (4 hours × $8)	32.00
Total production cost	83.00
Other overhead (20% × $83)	16.60
Total cost	99.60
Profit margin: 20% of sales (× 20/80)	24.90
Price to be quoted	124.50

10   The correct answer is: $12,383

	$
Salary costs: senior consultant (86 × $20)	1,720
junior time (220 × $15)	3,300
Overhead absorbed (306 hours × $12.50)	3,825
Total cost	8,845
Mark up (40%)	3,538
Selling price	12,383

If you selected the first option you did not include any absorbed overhead in your total cost. The second option is the total cost with no addition for profit, and if you selected the fourth option you calculated a 40% **margin** on the selling price, rather than a 40% **mark-up** on total cost.

11   The correct answer is: $34,500

	$
Salary costs: senior hours (3,000 × 1/4 × $20)	15,000
junior hours (3,000 × 3/4 × $15)	33,750
Overhead absorbed (3,000 hours × $12.50)	37,500
Total cost	86,250
Mark up (40%)	34,500

If you selected the second option you calculated a 40% margin based on the sales value, rather than on the cost. The third option is the total cost for the period and the fourth option is the total sales revenue for the period.

12   The correct answers are: Customer-driven production. Complete production possible within a single accounting period.

Each job is separately identifiable, according to a customer's requirements. Therefore the first characteristic is correct.

BPP LEARNING MEDIA

Jobs are usually of comparatively short duration, compared to situations where contract costing is applied. Therefore the second characteristic is correct.

The third characteristic is incorrect because each job is separately identifiable. The fourth characteristic applies to a batch.

13   The correct answer is: $72,761

The most logical basis for absorbing the overhead job costs is to use a percentage of direct labour cost.

$$\text{Overhead} = \frac{24,600}{(14,500 + 3,500 + 24,600)} \times \$126,000$$

$$= \frac{24,600}{42,600} \times \$126,000$$

$$= \$72,761$$

If you selected the first option you used the materials cost as the basis for overhead absorption. This would not be equitable because job number BB15 incurred no material cost and would therefore absorb no overhead. The second option is based on the prime cost of each job (material plus labour) and therefore suffers from the same disadvantage as the first option. The fourth option is the total overhead for the period, but some of this cost should be charged to the other two jobs.

14   The correct answer is: $84,963

	Job BB15
	$
Opening WIP	42,790
Labour for period	3,500
Overheads $\left(\dfrac{3,500}{42,600} \times 126,000\right)$	10,352
Total costs	56,642
Profit ($33^{1}/_{3}$% on sales = 50% costs)	28,321
	84,963

If you selected the first option you forgot to add on overhead cost. If you selected the second option you calculated the profit as 33% on cost, instead of 33% on sales. If you selected the fourth option you charged all of the overhead to job BBI5, but some of the overhead should be charged to the other two jobs.

15   The correct answer is: $217,323

Job number	WIP
	$
AA10 (26,800 + 17,275 + 14,500) + ($\dfrac{14,500}{42,600} \times 126,000$)	101,462
CC20 (18,500 + 24,600 + 72,761)	115,861
	217,323

The first option is the direct cost of job AA10, with no addition for overhead. The second option is the direct cost of both jobs in progress, but with no addition for overhead. The fourth option is the result of charging all of the overhead to the jobs in progress, but some of the overhead must be absorbed by the completed job BBI5.

13 Performance measures and service costing

1   The correct answer is: 1 and 2 only

In service costing it is difficult to identify many attributable direct costs. Many costs must be **shared over several cost units**, therefore characteristic 1 does apply. Composite cost units such as tonne-mile or room-night are often used, therefore characteristic 2 does apply. **Tangible** means 'touchable', such as a physical unit like a laptop, therefore characteristic 3 does not apply.

2   The correct answer is: 1 and 3 only

Cost per tonne-kilometre 1 is appropriate for cost control purposes because it **combines** the distance travelled and the load carried, **both of which affect cost**.

The fixed cost per kilometre 2 is not particularly useful for control purposes because it **varies with the number of kilometres travelled**.

The maintenance cost of each vehicle per kilometre 3 can be useful for control purposes because it **focuses on a particular aspect** of the cost of operating each vehicle.

3   The correct answer is: A light engineering company

All of the activities identified would use service costing, except the light engineering company which will be providing **products not services**.

4   The correct answer is: $1.50

The most appropriate cost unit is the **tonne-mile**. Therefore the cost per unit =

$$\frac{\$562,800}{375,200} = \$1.50$$

The first option is the cost per mile travelled. This is not as useful as the cost per tonne-mile, which **combines** the distance travelled and the load carried, **both of which affect cost**.

The third option is the cost per hour worked by drivers and the fourth option is the cost per driver employed. Costs are more likely to be incurred in relation to the distance travelled and the load carried.

5   The correct answers are: High levels of indirect costs as a proportion of total cost. Perishability. Use of composite cost units.

In service costing it is difficult to identify many attributable direct costs. Many costs must be treated as **indirect costs** and **shared over several cost units**, therefore the first characteristic does apply. Many services are **perishable**, for example a haircut or a cleaning service cannot be 'stored for later'. Therefore the second characteristic does apply. **Composite cost units** such as passenger-mile or bed-night are often used in service costing, therefore the third characteristic does apply. The fourth characteristic does not apply because services are usually heterogeneous.

6   The correct answers are: Vehicle cost per passenger-kilometre. Maintenance cost per vehicle per kilometre. Fuel cost per kilometre

The vehicle cost per passenger-kilometre is appropriate for cost control purposes because it **combines** the distance travelled and the number of passengers carried, **both of which affect cost**.

The maintenance cost for each vehicle per kilometre can be useful for control purposes because it **focuses on a particular aspect** of the cost of operating each vehicle.

The fixed cost per passenger is not particularly useful for control purposes because it **varies with the number of passengers carried**.

The fuel cost per kilometre can be useful for control purposes because it **focuses on a particular aspect** of resource consumption.

7   The correct answers are: Patient/day. Operating theatre hour. Outpatient visit.

All of the above would be **measurable** and would be **useful for control purposes**. A ward and an x-ray department are more likely to be used as **cost centres** for the purpose of cost collection and analysis.

8   The correct answer is:

Service	Cost unit
Hotels	D
Education	C
Hospitals	B
Catering organisations	A

9   The correct answer is: 16.67%

Gross profit is $25,500 × $21,250 = $4,250, which is 16.67% of $25,500.

10   The correct answer is: 10.71%

$$\frac{PBIT \times 100}{Capital} = \frac{1,200 \times 100}{11,200} = 10.71\%$$

11   The correct answer is: Achieving agreed targets

Effectiveness can only be measured in terms of achieved performance. Economy consists of minimising costs, for example, by obtaining suitable inputs at the lowest price. Efficiency, in the narrow sense used here, consists of achieving the greatest output per unit of input: avoiding waste of inputs would contribute to this. Achieving a given level of profit is a measure of overall efficiency in its wider sense and would require proper attention to all three of these matters. Profit is not a relevant performance measure for not for profit and public sector entities.

12   The correct answer is: Efficiency

Effectiveness can only be measured in terms of achieved performance. Economy consists of minimising costs, for example, by obtaining suitable inputs at the lowest price. Efficiency, in the narrow sense used here, consists of achieving the greatest output per unit of input.

13   The correct answer is:

	20X1	20X2
Net profit margin	12,000/80,000 = 15.0%	16,000/100,000 = 16.0%

14   The correct answer is:

	20X1	20X2
ROCE	12,000/60,000 = 20.0%	16,000/80,000 = 20.0%

15   The correct answer is:

	20X1	20X2
Asset turnover	80,000/60,000 = 1.33%	100,000/80,000 = 1.25%

14 Cost bookkeeping

1   The correct answer is: Debit: Overhead control account   Credit: Wages control account

Indirect costs of production, of which indirect wages are a part, are **'collected' as debits in the overhead control account**, from where they will eventually be **absorbed into work in progress**. The credit entry is made in the wages control account, where the wages cost has been 'collected' **prior to its analysis** between direct and indirect wages.

If you selected the first option you identified the correct accounts but your entries were reversed.

The second option represents the accounting entries for direct wages incurred, and the fourth option is the reverse of these entries.

2   The correct answer is:

	Debit	Credit
Work in progress account	70,800	
Overhead control account	2,500	
Wages control account		73,300

The overtime was not worked for any specific job and is therefore an **indirect wages cost** to be 'collected' in the overhead control account. Similarly, the holiday pay is an **indirect cost**, therefore the total **debit to the overhead control account** is $2,500. The **direct wages** of $70,800 is **debited to the work in progress account** and the total wages cost is **credited to the wages control account**.

If you selected the third option you identified the correct accounts but your entries were reversed.

If you selected the first option you treated the overtime premium as a direct cost, and if you selected the fourth option you made the same mistake and your entries were reversed.

3   The correct answer is: Wages for February were prepaid by $12,000.

The credit balance on the wages control account indicates that the amount of wages incurred and analysed between direct wages and indirect wages was **higher** than the wages paid through the bank. Therefore there was a $12,000 balance of **wages owing** at the end of February and statement two is not correct.

The first option is correct. $128,400 of wages was paid from the bank account.

The third option is correct. $79,400 of direct wages was transferred to the work in progress control account.

The fourth option is correct. $61,000 of indirect wages was transferred to the production overhead control account.

4   The correct answer is: Debit: Raw material price variance account   Credit: Raw material control account

The situation described results in an **adverse** raw material price variance and therefore a **debit** to the raw material price variance account. This eliminates the first two options. The price variance is **eliminated where it arises**, ie on receipt into materials inventory, therefore the credit entry is made in the raw material control account.

5   The correct answer is: Debit: Work in progress control account   Credit: Labour efficiency variance account

A **favourable** labour efficiency variance is **credited** to the labour efficiency variance account. This eliminates the first and last options.

The efficiency variance is **eliminated where it arises** therefore the debit entry is made in the work in progress account.

6   The correct answer is: Debit: Work in progress control account   Credit: Material usage variance account

A favourable variance is credited in the relevant variance account. The usage variance is eliminated where it arises, therefore the debit entry is made in the work-in-progress account.

7   The correct answers are:

	Debit	Credit	No entry in this account
Raw materials control account	✓		
WIP control account			✓
Raw material price variance account		✓	

When materials are purchased for more or less than their standard price, the variance is debited or credited respectively to the material price variance account.

8   The correct answer is: Debit: Wages control account   Credit: Labour rate variance account

A **favourable** labour rate variance is **credited** to the labour rate variance account. This eliminates the first and third options.

The rate variance is **eliminated where it arises**, ie on payment of the wages, therefore the debit entry is made in the wages control account.

9   The correct answer is: Debit: Material usage variance account   Credit: Work in progress control account

An **adverse** material usage variance is **debited** to the material usage variance account. This eliminates the third and fourth options.

The usage variance is **eliminated where it arises**, therefore the credit entry is made in the work in progress account.

10   The correct answer is: Debit: Finished goods control account   Credit: Work in progress control account

The factory cost of finished production is transferred as a debit to the **finished goods account** and **credited from the work in progress account**.

11   The correct answers are:

	Debit	Credit	No entry in this account
Overhead control account	✓		
Work in progress account			✓
Statement of profit or loss		✓	

If overheads are over-absorbed, this means that there is too much expense in the statement of profit or loss so we need to credit the statement of profit or loss.

12   The correct answer is: DR work in progress control account; CR stores control account

Direct costs of production are **debited to the work in progress account**. Direct materials are taken from stores and therefore the credit will be in the **stores control account**.

The second option is incorrect because **all production costs must be collected in the work in progress account** before the transfer of the cost of completed output to the finished goods account.

The third option has the correct entries, but they are reversed.

The fourth option is incorrect because a **transfer to cost of sales cannot be made until the cost of production has been determined**.

13   The correct answer is: Debit: Work in progress account $81,000   Credit: Overhead control account $81,000

Overhead absorbed = 27,000 hours × $3 = $81,000. This amount is **debited in the work in progress account** as part of the cost of production for the period. The credit entry is made in the **overhead control account**.

If you selected the first option you identified the correct accounts but you used the figure for **actual overheads incurred**. The second option is incorrect because the cost of production must first be 'collected' in the **work in progress account** before the final transfer of the cost of completed production to the finished goods account. The fourth option uses the correct values and accounts, but the **entries are reversed**.

14   The correct answer is: Debit: Statement of profit or loss $4,000   Credit: Overhead control account $4,000

	$
Overhead absorbed	81,000
Overhead incurred	85,000
Under-absorbed overhead	4,000

This means that the overhead charged to production was too low therefore there must be a **debit to statement of profit or loss**. The credit entry is made in the **overhead control account**.

The second option demonstrates the entries for **over-absorbed overhead**.

The third and fourth options are incorrect because under or over absorption of overhead does not affect work in progress (WIP). The only overhead charge made to WIP is the **overhead absorbed based on the predetermined rate**.

15   The correct answer is:

Debit   Work in progress control account   116,900
Credit   Stores ledger control account   116,900

The easiest way to solve this question is to draw up a stores ledger control account.

STORES LEDGER CONTROL ACCOUNT

	$		$
Opening inventory b/f	18,500	Suppliers (returns)	2,300
Suppliers/cash (deliveries)	142,000	Overhead account (indirect materials)	25,200
		WIP (balancing figure)	116,900
		Closing inventory c/f	16,100
	160,500		160,500

If you selected the third option you determined the correct value of the direct materials issued but you **reversed the entries**.

If you selected the first or second options you omitted the figure for returns, and in the first option you **reversed the entries** for the issue of direct materials from stores.

15 Risk and probability

1   The correct answer is: 0.44

Probability of A or B occurring = P(A) + P(B), provided A and B cannot both be true, so P(sales remaining the same or falling)
= P(same) + P(falling)
= 0.21 + 0.23
= 0.44

2   The correct answer is: 0.92

P(male)   = 40% =   0.4
P(female)   = 1 – 0.4 =   0.6
P(CIMA candidate) = 80% = 0.8

We need to use the general rule of addition (to avoid double counting)

P(female or CIMA candidate)
= P(female) + P(CIMA candidate) – P(female and CIMA candidate)
= 0.6 + 0.8 – (0.6 × 0.8) = 0.92

3   The correct answer is: 0.42

	L	W
P(sale)	0.3	0.4
P(no sale)	0.7	0.6

Pr(no sale at L and W) = 0.7 × 0.6 = 0.42

4   The correct answer is: 0.835

P(at least one sale) = 1 – Pr(no sales)
P(no sales)   = (0.6 × 0.55 × 0.5) = 0.165
P(at least one sale) = 1 – 0.165
                      = 0.835

5   The correct answer is: 0.40

	Given low-fat food	Given normal food	Total
Lost weight	200	250	450
No weight loss	300	250	550
	500	500	1,000

Pr (dog has lost weight given that it received low-fat food) $= \dfrac{200}{500} = 0.40$

6   The correct answer is: Statement 1 and 2

These statements both define an expected value.

7   The correct answer is: An EV is inappropriate if decisions are being constantly repeated.

An EV is more appropriate where a decision is being repeated because it should ensure optimal decision making over the long-term.

EVs are inappropriate for one-off decisions, and where probabilities used when calculating expected values are likely to be unreliable or inaccurate; EVs ignore risk where risk is the spread or variability of outcomes.

8   The correct answer is: $11,500

EV = (15,000 × 0.2) + (20,000 × 0.5) + (– 5,000 × 0.3)
= 3,000 + 10,000 – 1,500
= 11,500

9   The correct answer is: Project Beta

Expected value of Project Alpha

(0.5 × $50,000) + (0.5 × $20,000) = $25,000 + $10,000 = $35,000

Expected value of Project Beta

(0.6 × $60,000) + (0.4 × $10,000) = $36,000 + $4,000 = $40,000

Project Beta should therefore be chosen since it generates the highest expected profits of $40,000.

10   The correct answer is: –$75

Current expected value

(0.6 × $3,000) + (0.4 × $1,500)   = $1,800 + $600
                                  = $2,400

Revised expected value

(0.55 × $3,000) + (0.45 × $1,500) = $1,650 + $675
                                  = $2,325

There is therefore a fall of $75.

11   The correct answer is: 3%

Pr(sale)   = 0.8
Pr(no sale) = 0.2
Pr(sale on third call) = P (no sale, no sale, sale)
                        = 0.2 × 0.2 × 0.8
                        = 0.032
                        = 3%

12   The correct answer is: 0.25

We can calculate the required probability by using the values calculated in the following contingency table.

	Pay	Default	Total
Check	36	4	40
No check	48	12	60
Total	84	16	100

Workings

No check   = 60% of 100 = 60
Check   = 100 – 60   = 40
No check but pay = 80% of 60 = 48
Check, pay   = 90% of 40 = 36

The other figures are balancing figures. P(customer checked-defaults) = 4/16 = 0.25

13   The correct answer is: 0.25

	Age of customer		
	Under 21	21 and over	Total
Expenditure			
Under $25	55	205	260
$25 to $50	125	80	205
Over $50	10	25	35
	190	310	500

Number of customers under 21 spending between $25 and $50 is 125. Therefore, the probability that a customer is under 21 **and** spent between $25 and $50 is:

$$\frac{125}{500} = 0.25$$

14   The correct answer is: 0.66

We can rephrase this question to 'given that a customer is aged under 21, what is the probability that he spent between $25 and $50?'

Instead of being concerned with the whole sample (500) we are only concerned with those who are under 21 (190).

The table shows that 125 under 21 year olds spent between $25 and $50.

$\therefore$ P (Customer under 21 spent $25 – $50) = $\frac{125}{190}$ = 0.66

15   The correct answer is: 0.61

We can rephrase this question to 'given that a customer spent between $25 and $50, what is the probability that they are aged under 21?'

Number of customers spending between $25 and $50 = 205, of which 125 are under 21 years.

$\therefore$ P (Customer spending between $25 and $50 is under 21) = $\dfrac{125}{205}$ = 0.61

16   The correct answer is: Choice 4.

EV of Choice 1 = $9,500

EV of Choice 2 = $(0.3 \times 14,000) + (0.3 \times 10,000) + (0.4 \times 5,000)$ = $9,200

EV of Choice 3 = $(0.4 \times 10,000) + (0.6 \times 9,000)$ = $9,400

EV of Choice 4 = $(0.7 \times 8,000) + (0.3 \times 14,000)$ = $9,800

16 Averages and the normal distribution

1   The correct answer is: 78.35

25% of normal frequencies will occur between the mean and the upper quartile. From normal distribution tables, 25% of frequencies lie between the mean and a point approximately 0.67 standard deviations above the mean.

The standard deviation is the square root of the variance and is $\sqrt{25}$ = 5 in this case.

The upper quartile is therefore 0.67 × 5 = 3.35 above the mean. The upper quartile = 3.35 + 75 = 78.35.

You should have been able to eliminate the first two options straightaway since 58.25 and 71.65 are below the mean. The upper quartile of any distribution will be above the mean. The second option represents the lower quartile (75 – 3.35).

If you had forgotten to take the square root of the variance in order to obtain the standard deviation, you would have calculated the upper quartile as being 0.67 × 25 = 16.75 above the mean, ie 75 + 16.75 = 91.75. The fourth option is therefore also incorrect for this reason.

2   The correct answer is: Median

Sample 1 median = average of second and third items in the array, ie

$$\left(\dfrac{5+5}{2}\right) = 5$$

Sample 2 median = the middle (third) item in the array, ie 5. The median has the same value, therefore, in both samples.

3   The correct answer is: 7,000

Firstly, we need to calculate the cumulative frequency of earnings.

Annual earnings $	Frequency	Cumulative frequency
6,000	3	3
7,000	5	8
10,000	3	11
11,000	1	12
12,000	2	14
15,000	1	15

The median is the $(15 + 1)/2$ = 8th item which has a value of $7,000.

4   The correct answer is: 160

Number of employees in department 2 = 100 – 54 – 24 = 22. For all employees, mean output per month = 139. Let x = the mean output per employee per month for department 2.

$$
\begin{aligned}
139 &= [(54 \times 130) + (22 \times x) + (24 \times 140)]/100 \\
139 \times 100 &= 7,020 + 22x + 3,360 \\
13,900 &= 10,380 + 22x \\
22x &= 13,900 - 10,380 \\
x &= 3,520/22 \\
x &= \mathbf{160}
\end{aligned}
$$

5   The correct answer is: Mean weight kg: 300   Standard deviation kg: 30

Mean of A + B + C = (120 + 100 + 80)kg = 300 kg

Variance of A + B + C = (400 + 400 + 100) = 900 kg

(However, don't forget to calculate the square root of 900 in order to calculate the standard deviation as required by the question.) Standard deviation   = √variance
                                                                            = √900 = 30 kg

Packets of one of each of A, B and C have a mean weight of 300 kg and a standard deviation of 30 kg. If you selected the first option, you forgot that the overall means should have been added together.

If you selected the second option you forgot to add the means together, and you also forgot to take the square root of the variance in order to calculate the standard deviation.

If you selected the fourth option, you forgot to take the square root of the variance in order to calculate the standard deviation.

6   The correct answer is: 20%

B   Coefficient of variation = standard deviation/mean
                                              = 1/5
                                              = 20%

7   The correct answer is: 13.7

$$\text{Standard deviation} = \sqrt{\frac{\Sigma fx^2}{\Sigma f} - \bar{x}^2} \text{ where } \bar{x} = \frac{\Sigma fx}{\Sigma f}$$

$$= \sqrt{\frac{61,250}{50} - \left(\frac{1,610}{50}\right)^2}$$

$$= \sqrt{1,225 - 32.2^2}$$

$$= \sqrt{188.16}$$

$$= 13.7$$

8   The correct answer is: 2.2

$\Sigma fx = (10 \times 1) + (10 \times 2) + (20 \times 3) + (5 \times 4) = 110$ rejects
$\Sigma f = 50$

Rejects per sample $= \Sigma fx/\Sigma = 110/50 = 2.2$

9   The correct answer is: 25%

$$\text{Coefficient of variation} = \text{standard deviation/mean}$$
$$= 3/12$$
$$= 25\%$$

10   The correct answer is: 8%

$\mu = 50$ cm
$\sigma = 5$ cm
$z = (57 - 50)/5 = 1.4$

Using normal distribution tables, the proportion between the mean and 1.4 standard deviations above the mean = 0.4192

∴ The percentage of tubes at least 57 cm long is $(0.5 - 0.4192) = 0.0808 = 8.08\%$

The percentage is closest to 8%.

The second option, 42% represents the proportion of tubes between 50 and 57 cm long.

The third option, 58% represents the proportion of tubes below the mean and above 57 cm.

The fourth option represents the proportion of tubes below 57 cm.

11   The correct answer is: 98 g

Probability of weight being between the mean of 400 and 450 = 39/2 = 19.5%

From normal distribution tables, 19.5% of frequencies lie between the mean and a point 0.51 standard deviations above the mean (ie our z score is 0.51).

$$\text{If } z = \frac{x - \mu}{\sigma}$$

$$0.51 = \frac{450 - 400}{\sigma}$$

$$\sigma = 50/0.51 = 98$$

BPP
LEARNING
MEDIA

12 The correct answer is: 0.15

P(score > 59) = $P(z > \dfrac{59-55}{\sqrt{14.44}})$ = P(z >1.05) = 0.5 − 0.3531 = 0.1469

= 0.15 approx

13 The correct answer is: 30

We need to put the numbers in order and find the middle value. As there are 9 numbers, the middle value will be the 5th number.

23, 25, 25, 30, 30, 31, 31, 31, 35

The 5th number is 30.

14 The correct answer is: 31

The mode is the most common time, ie 31, as 31 occurs three times in the list.

15 The correct answer is: 29

We add up all of the times and divide by the number of results (ie 9).

(23 + 25 + 25 + 30 + 30 + 31 + 31 + 31 + 35)/9 = 261/9 =29

16 The correct answer is: Area

A histogram is a chart that looks like a bar chart except that the bars are joined together. On a histogram, frequencies are represented by the area covered by the bars (compare this with a bar chart where the frequencies are represented by the heights of the bars).

17 The correct answer is: A simple bar chart

The best diagram to draw to highlight the differences between areas is a simple bar chart .

A simple bar chart is a chart consisting of one or more bars, in which the length of each bar indicates the magnitude of the corresponding data items. This is the best diagram to draw to highlight the differences of typical salaries in different areas.

We are not interested in showing the breakdown of the total salary, therefore a pie diagram and a percentage component bar chart are not really appropriate.

A multiple bar chart is a bar chart in which two or more separate bars are used to present sub-divisions of data. The data available relating to salaries is not subdivided and this type of chart is therefore not appropriate in this situation.

18 $105,000

$630,000 × (60/360) = $105,000

17 Investment appraisal

1   The correct answer is: $1,800 in exactly four years from now

       PV of $1,200 in one year = $1,200 × 0.926 = 1,111.20
       PV of $1,400 in two years = $1,400 × 0.857 = 1,199.80
       PV of $1,600 in three years = $1,600 × 0.794 = 1,270.40
       PV of $1,800 in four years = $1,800 × 0.735 = 1,323.00

2   The correct answer is: 9.85%

       The formula to calculate the IRR is $a\% + \left[\dfrac{A}{A-B} \times (b-a) \right]\%$

       where a = one interest rate
              b = other interest rate
              A = NPV at rate a
              B = NPV at rate b

       $\text{IRR} = 9\% + \left[\dfrac{22}{22+4} \times 1 \right]\%$
             $= 9 + 0.85 = 9.85\%$

       If you selected the first option you took it to be 'the other interest rate', and you subtracted the 0.85 instead of adding it.

       You should have spotted that the third and fourth options were invalid because if the NPV is positive at one rate and negative at another rate, the IRR will be somewhere between the two rates, ie between 9% and 10%.

3   The correct answer is: Accept if the present value of future cash flows is positive

       Accept the project if the net present value is positive

4   The correct answer is: $38,328

       Present value = $8,000 + ($8,000 × 3.791) = $38,328

5   The correct answer is: $5,073

       Annuity = $700

       Annuity factor = 1 + 6.247 (cumulative factor for 9 years, first payment is now) = 7.247

       Annuity   = PV of annuity/annuity factor

       $700   = PV of annuity/7.247

       PV of annuity = $5,073 (to the nearest $)

6   The correct answer is: Between 10% and 15%

	$
Investment	(60,000)
PV of cash inflow	64,600
NPV @ 10%	4,600

	$
Investment	(60,000)
PV of cash inflow	58,200
NPV @ 15%	(1,800)

The IRR of the machine investment is therefore between 10% and 15% because the NPV falls from $4,600 at 10% to – $1,800 at 15%. Therefore at some point between 10% and 15% the NPV = 0. When the NPV = 0, the internal rate of return is reached.

7   The correct answer is: $61,016

Let x = investment at start of project.

Year	Cash flow $	Discount factor 10%	Present value $
0	x	1.000	(x)
1–5	18,000	3.791	68,238
			7,222

$\therefore$ – x + $68,238 = $7,222

x = $68,238 – $7,222

x = $61,016

8   The correct answer is: Statement 2 only

Statement 1 is not true. Payback is fairly easy to understand. Statement 2 is true and is a disadvantage of payback. Statement 3 is not true. Payback only takes account of the cash flows up to the point of payback.

9   The correct answer is: 1, 2 and 4 only

The following problems arise when using net present values to appraise an investment.

- Estimating future cash flows
- Selecting an appropriate discount rate
- Non-accountants often find it difficult to understand the concept of net present value

Inflation will often be ignored when two alternative investments are being considered since both will be affected by it. 3 is therefore not (generally) a problem with the use of net present values in appraising projects.

10   The correct answer is: 12.5%

Using the formula:

IRR = 2 + (35,000/(35,000 – 15,000) $\times$ (8 – 2)) = 12.5%

11 The correct answer is: $333

A four year payback period implies an (equal) annual cash flow of $12,000 ÷ 4 years = $3,000 per year. As these cash flows run for 6 years the NPV is equal to $333 (– $12,000 + annuity factor for 6 years @ 12% × $3,000 = –$12,000 + 4.111 × $3,000 = $333).

The third option is based upon an incorrect calculation of annual cash flow ($12,000 ÷ 6 years = $2,000 per year), suggesting a misunderstanding of the payback method.

In the second option the NPV was based on a project life of 4 years rather than 6, suggesting a failure to read the question carefully.

Finally the fourth option's NPV was based upon a combination of the other two distracters; that is, an annual cash flow of $2,000 for 4 years.

12 The correct answer is: 2 years and 10 months

The net cash flows of the project are:

Year 1	(89,500)
Year 2	(44,000)
Year 3	8,000

Therefore the machine pays back between years 2 and 3.

Assuming the cash flows accrue evenly during the year, the machine will pay back

$\left(\dfrac{\$44,000}{\$52,000}\right) \times 12 = 10$ months into the year.

Therefore the payback period is 2 years and 10 months.

13 The correct answer is: 2 years and 6 months

Workings

Year	Cash inflow	Cumulative cash inflow
	$	$
1	250,000	250,000
2	350,000	600,000
3	400,000	1,000,000
4	200,000	1,200,000
5	150,000	1,350,000
6	150,000	1,500,000

The project has a payback period of between 2 and 3 years.

Payback period $= 2 \text{ years} + \left[\dfrac{\$200,000}{\$400,000} \times 12 \text{ months}\right]$

$= 2 \text{ years} + 6 \text{ months}$

14   The correct answer is: $331,100

Year	Cash inflow	Cumulative cash inflow	Cumulative cash inflow
	$	$	$
0	(800,000)	1.000	−800,000
1	250,000	0.909	227,250
2	350,000	0.826	289,100
3	400,000	0.751	300,400
4	200,000	0.683	136,600
5	150,000	0.621	93,150
6	150,000	0.564	84,600
		NPV =	331,100

15   The correct answer is: 25.4%

$$\text{IRR} = 20\% + \left(\frac{89{,}700}{89{,}700 + 77{,}024} \times (30 - 20) \right)\%$$

$$= 20\% + 5.4\%$$

$$= 25.4\%$$

16   The correct answers are:

Ignores the time value of money	**Payback**
Discount rate that gives a NPV of zero	**IRR**
Accept project if appraisal method gives a positive figure	**NPV**
Most important investment criterion	**NPV**

Mock exam questions

1   BGY Co invested in a new machine that cost of $30,000 when purchased.

The company has calculated the following net present values of the expected net cash inflows over the machine's useful life.

Discount rate	Present value of cash inflows
%	$
10	34,500
15	32,200
20	29,400

What is the internal rate of return (IRR) of the machine investment?

○   Below 10%
○   Between 10% and 15%
○   Between 15% and 20%
○   Over 20%

2   GHU Co's management accounts for last month showed the following results:

	Fixed budget	Flexed budget	Actual results
	$	$	$
Direct costs	250,500	264,255	265,130
Production overhead	300,000	312,700	310,950
Other overhead	50,000	52,150	55,750
	600,500	629,105	631,830

Calculate the adverse expenditure variance for the month. $ [   ]

3   ZYB Co absorbs overheads using a direct machine hour rate.

In the last period, budgeted production overheads were $230,000 and actual production overheads amounted to $232,725. Actual machine hours were 57,500. Production overheads were under-absorbed by $12,500.

Calculate the overhead absorption rate per machine hour.

$ [   ]

4   **Which of the following describes a standard hour?**

○   An hour during which budgeted labour and machine hours are achieved.

○   An hour used to measure the total amount of output that is achievable in the time, when working at standard efficiency levels.

○   An hour where only identical units are made.

○   An hour where no exceptional events occur.

BPP
LEARNING
MEDIA

5   In its latest management accounts, XYZ Co has a favourable material price variance.

Which of the following explains the cause of the variance?

○   An error in calculating the standard price of direct material that resulted in a figure which is too high.
○   The purchase of better quality material than standard.
○   The purchase of more material than budgeted.
○   The loss of bulk discounts on materials purchased.

6   GTR Co wishes to minimise the risk of its credit customers failing to pay what they owe. It has recently instructed a credit rating agency to check the rating of its customers. GTR Co's management decided that only customers that are rated as a good credit risk would be offered credit.

The credit rating agency reported that 80% of GTR Co customers that it rated as a good credit risk paid their debts without a problem.

In terms of potential customers, the credit rating agency reported that in its experience, 70% of people that are granted credit without a credit check pay their debts without difficulty. 50% of people are not checked by the credit rating agency.

Calculate the probability that a customer who defaults was checked by a credit rating agency is (to 2 decimal places):

[   ]

7   **State which of the following are characteristics of service costing.**

1   High levels of indirect costs as a proportion of total costs.
2   Use of composite cost units.
3   Tangible units of production.

○   1 only
○   1 and 2 only
○   2 only
○   2 and 3 only

8   **Which of the following are relevant costs for decision making?**

Select all that apply.

☐   Avoidable costs.
☐   Future committed costs.
☐   Opportunity costs.
☐   Differential costs.

9   Hill Co has recently started manufacturing a new product, TG15. The product's selling price is to be set at a figure which achieves a 20% return on investment.

The following information is available regarding TG15.

Material cost per unit	$12.50
Labour cost per unit	$28.60
Production overhead cost per machine hour	$5.50
Machine hours per unit	3
General overhead absorption rate	15% of total production cost
Annual capital investment	$1,674,750
Annual production (units)	15,000

Calculate the selling price per unit of the TG15 to the nearest $0.01:

$ [   ]

---

10   XYZ Co absorbs overheads on the basis of labour hours.

Budgeted labour hours were 14,575 with budgeted overheads of $641,300.

Actual results were 14,359 labour hours and overheads of $640,375.

Overheads were:

○   Under absorbed by $8,579
○   Over absorbed by $925
○   Under absorbed by $925
○   Over absorbed by $8,579

---

11   Jay Co's budgeted figures for last month are shown below.

	Budget
Production/sales units	20,000
	$
Direct material	55,000
Direct labour	40,000
Variable overhead	30,000
Fixed overhead	35,000
Sales revenue	275,000

The company uses a marginal costing system and all direct costs are wholly variable.

It is expecting to sell 24,000 units next month.

Calculate the flexed budget profit for next month.

$ [   ]

BPP
LEARNING
MEDIA

12 **What is a basic standard?**

   ○ A standard that includes no allowance for losses, waste and inefficiencies. It represents the level of performance that is attainable under perfect operating conditions.

   ○ A standard that includes some allowance for losses, waste and inefficiencies. It represents the level of performance that is attainable under efficient operating conditions.

   ○ A standard that is based on currently attainable operating conditions.

   ○ A standard that is kept unchanged, to show the trend in costs.

---

13 **Which of the following is NOT included in a batch cost?**

   ☐ Actual material cost
   ☐ Actual manufacturing overheads
   ☐ Absorbed manufacturing overheads
   ☐ Actual labour cost

---

14 Raz Co operates a chain of night clubs in major cities around the country. Over one month it recorded the length of time people had to queue to enter each club. The company found that the mean queuing time was 10 minutes with a standard deviation of 0.5 minutes.

   Calculate the coefficient of variation as a percentage.

   ☐ %

---

15 **Which TWO of the following statements about the payback method of investment appraisal are correct?**

   ☐ Payback is a fairly easy technique to understand.
   ☐ Payback ignores the time value of money.
   ☐ Payback takes into account all of an investment's lifetime cash flows.
   ☐ Payback is only valid for investments with a life over five years.

---

16 **Which THREE of the following statements describe a professional, according to IFAC's definition of the role and domain of the professional accountant in business?**

   ☐ Someone subject to oversight by a body with disciplinary powers.

   ☐ Someone committed to the values of accuracy, honesty, integrity, objectivity, transparency and reliability.

   ☐ Someone with skills, knowledge and expertise tested by examination and continuously developed in a structured and monitored context.

   ☐ Someone bound by a system of ethical rules.

---

17 Management accountants often work in public services such as health or education. The information that the management accountant provides an organisation depends on its objectives.

Which of the following is an objective of a public service organisation?

○ To employ a certain number of staff
○ To generate a certain return on investment
○ To hold a certain amount of working capital
○ To operate at a certain level of efficiency

---

18 The following data is available for a factory.

Total cost of production	Volume of production
$	Units
35,000	1,500
47,600	2,200

Calculate the factory's total fixed cost.

Select the correct option.

○ $8,000
○ $20,600
○ $12,600
○ $27,000

---

19 Lec Co designs and builds electronic components that are used in smart phones and tablet computers. The following information is available concerning the standard cost of one of its products, the FT57.

	$
Direct material	4.25
Direct labour	3.50
Variable overhead	1.75
Fixed overhead absorption rate	9.50
	19.00
Profit	5.00
Selling price	24.00

Budgeted production last month was 50,000 units, but actual production exceeded this amount at 57,500 units. Lec Co sold 52,500 of these units. At the start of the month, the company had no units in its opening inventory. Fixed overhead costs incurred during the month were $545,000.

Calculate the marginal costing profit for the month to the nearest $1.

$ [   ]

20   Lec Co designs and builds electronic components that are used in smart phones and tablet computers. The following information is available concerning the standard cost of one of its products, the FT57.

	$
Direct material	4.25
Direct labour	3.50
Variable overhead	1.75
Fixed overhead absorption rate	9.50
	19.00
Profit	5.00
Selling price	24.00

Budgeted production last month was 50,000 units, but actual production exceeded this amount at 57,500 units. Lec Co sold 52,500 of these units. At the start of the month, the company had no units in its opening inventory.

Fixed overhead costs incurred during the month were $545,000.

Calculate the absorption costing profit for the month to the nearest $1.

$ [   ]

---

21   Lec Co designs and builds electronic components that are used in smart phones and tablet computers. The following information is available concerning the standard cost of one of its products, the FT57.

	$
Direct material	4.25
Direct labour	3.50
Variable overhead	1.75
Fixed overhead absorption rate	9.50
	19.00
Profit	5.00
Selling price	24.00

Budgeted production last month was 50,000 units, but actual production exceeded this amount at 57,500 units. Lec Co sold 52,500 of these units. At the start of the month, the company had no units in its opening inventory.

Fixed overhead costs incurred during the month were $545,000.

How did the profit for the month compare under marginal costing and absorption costing?

O   Profit under absorption costing was higher than under marginal costing by $47,500.
O   Profit under marginal costing was higher than under absorption costing by $47,500.
O   Profit under absorption costing was higher than under marginal costing by $251,750.
O   Profit under marginal costing was higher than under absorption costing by $251,750.

---

22   James is considering the purchase of a $2,000 perpetuity in a year's time. Interest rates are currently 5%.

What price should James pay for the perpetuity, to the nearest $1?

O $2,100
O $30,100
O $40,000
O $42,300

23 **Which of the following is NOT one of the three E's used to describe the objectives of public sector organisations?**

○   Efficiency
○   Externality
○   Effectiveness
○   Economy

24 Brew Co bottles a range of soft drinks. Each bottle has a capacity of 1 litre. During the bottling process 5% of the liquid input is lost due to spillage. The standard cost of the liquid is $1.50 per litre.

Calculate the standard cost of the liquid per bottle, to the nearest $0.01.

$ [   ]

25 The following is a profit-volume chart for Product X.

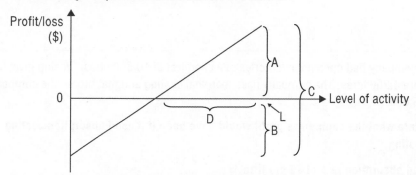

Which of the following distances indicates the contribution at level of activity L?

○   Distance A
○   Distance B
○   Distance C
○   Distance D

26 **Which of the following costs does the graph depict?**

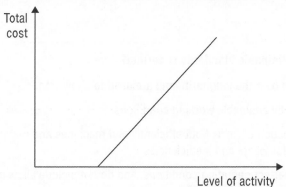

○   A utility bill with fixed and variable cost elements.
○   An employee's bonus of $5 per unit for every unit above 100 units
○   The rental cost of office space.
○   Costs of material used in a factory process.

27 The following information is available regarding the four cost centres of AB Co.

	Grinding	Assembly	Polishing	Service cost centre canteen
			Production Cost Centres	
Number of direct employees	10	15	9	-
Number of indirect employees	5	12	2	8
Overhead allocated and apportioned	$79,575	$89,150	$39,750	$12,000

The overhead cost of the canteen is to be re-apportioned to the production cost centres on the basis of the number of employees in each production cost centre.

Calculate the total overhead cost of the assembly department (to the nearest $) after the service cost centre costs are re-allocated.

- ○ $6,113
- ○ $94,461
- ○ $94,444
- ○ $95,263

---

28 In a particular month, a company had opening inventories of a chemical of 10,500 litres. Closing inventories of the same chemical were 4,250 litres. The company uses marginal costing and that month the company achieved a profit of $125,000.

To the nearest $, calculate what the company's profit would have been if it used absorption costing rather than marginal costing.

Assume a fixed overhead absorption rate of $5 per litre.

[   ]

---

29 A company is facing an unexpected, temporary cash shortage.

Which of the following is an appropriate course of action for the company to take?

- ○ Contact the bank to arrange an overdraft.
- ○ Demand early repayment from customers.
- ○ Pay suppliers early.
- ○ Increase production.

---

30 **Which of the following statements regarding attainable standards is correct?**

- ○ Attainable standards are designed for use over the long term, and are used to show trends.

- ○ Attainable standards are based on currently attainable working conditions.

- ○ Attainable standards are attained if production is carried out efficiently and machines and materials are used properly. Allowances are made for waste and inefficiencies.

- ○ Attainable standards are attained under perfect operating conditions, and do not include allowances for wastage, spoilage, machine breakdowns and other inefficiencies.

---

31   XYC Co manufactures a single product (TP39). The company's factory operates at 75% capacity which is the normal level of activity.

The product has a selling price of $10 and sales are $600,000 per month.

Direct cost per unit	$3
Production overhead	$156,000 (including variable costs of $30,000)
Sales costs	$80,000
Distribution costs	$60,000 (including variable costs of $15,000)
Administration overhead	$40,000 (including variable costs of $9,000)

The sales costs are fixed with the exception of sales commission, which is 5% of sales value.

Calculate the contribution per unit.

$ [   ]

---

32   XYC Co manufactures a single product (TP39). The company's factory operates at 75% capacity which is the normal level of activity.

The product has a selling price of $10 and sales are $600,000 per month.

Direct cost per unit	$3
Production overhead	$156,000 (including variable costs of $30,000)
Sales costs	$80,000
Distribution costs	$60,000 (including variable costs of $15,000)
Administration overhead	$40,000 (including variable costs of $9,000)

The sales costs are fixed with the exception of sales commission, which is 5% of sales value.

Calculate the fixed cost per month.

$ [   ]

---

33   XYC Co manufactures a single product (TP39). The company's factory operates at 75% capacity which is the normal level of activity.

The product has a selling price of $10 and sales are $600,000 per month.

Direct cost per unit	$3
Production overhead	$156,000 (including variable costs of $30,000)
Sales costs	$80,000
Distribution costs	$60,000 (including variable costs of $15,000)
Administration overhead	$40,000 (including variable costs of $9,000)

The sales costs are fixed with the exception of sales commission, which is 5% of sales value.

Calculate the breakeven volume of sales per month in units.

The breakeven volume of sales per month is [   ] units

34   **Which THREE of the following are functional budgets?**

☐   Statement of financial position budget
☐   Sales budget
☐   Material cost budget
☐   Advertising budget
☐   Cash budget

---

35   A company operates a standard costing system where inventory is valued at standard cost. One of its processes uses Chemical X which has a standard cost of $0.40 per litre.

Last month, the company purchased 10,000 litres of Chemical X for a price of $4,250 and used 7,800 litres in production.

What is the direct material price variance for last month?

○ $195 (A)
○ $195 (F)
○ $250 (A)
○ $250 (F)

---

36   **Job costing is appropriate to use in which TWO of the following situations?**

☐   Where production is expected to run over several accounting periods
☐   Where production operates continuously
☐   Where production is for a single special order
☐   Where production of the product lasts for a relatively short time

---

37   Juno Co has decided to lease a printing machine. Under the terms of the lease, the company will make five annual payments of $10,000. The first payment will be made when the machine is delivered next week. The following is an extract from an annuity table:

Year	Annuity factor 10%
1	0.909
2	1.736
3	2.487
4	3.170
5	3.791
6	4.355

What is the present value of the lease payments at an interest rate of 10%?

○ $31,700
○ $37,910
○ $41,700
○ $47,910

38   A company is considering investing in a new project, Beta 12 and uses a discount rate of 8% when appraising new projects.

The project's cash flows are as follows:

Year	Cashflow ($)
0	(100,000)
1	35,000
2	35,000
3	35,000
4	35,000

The following extracts from annuity tables are available.

Year	Annuity factor 8%
1	0.926
2	1.783
3	2.577
4	3.312
5	3.993

Which of the following describes how the project's payback period is calculated?

○   Initial investment ÷ annual profit
○   Initial investment ÷ annual net cash inflow
○   (Initial investment – residual value) ÷ annual profit
○   (Initial investment – residual value) ÷ annual net cash inflow

---

39   A company is considering investing in a new project, Beta 12 and uses a discount rate of 8% when appraising new projects. The project's cash flows are as follows:

Year	Cashflow ($)
0	(100,000)
1	35,000
2	35,000
3	35,000
4	35,000

The following extracts from annuity tables are available.

Year	Annuity factor 8%
1	0.926
2	1.783
3	2.577
4	3.312
5	3.993

Calculate the net present value (NPV) of the project.

$ [   ]

BPP
LEARNING
MEDIA

40 **Indicate whether the following characteristics relate to strategic or operational level information.**

	(i) Strategic-level information	(ii) Operational-level information
a. Forward looking	☐	☐
b. Historical	☐	☐
c. Externally focused	☐	☐
d. Internally focused	☐	☐
e. Relevant to the long-term	☐	☐
f. Relevant to the short-term	☐	☐

41

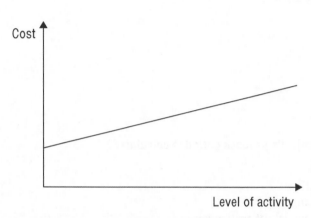

Which type of cost does the graph depict?

○ Fixed cost
○ Variable cost
○ Stepped cost
○ Mixed cost

42 ABC Co reapportions service department costs using the repeated distribution method.

Which of the following statements regarding ABC Co is correct?

○ ABC Co has more service departments than production cost centres.

○ ABC Co's service departments carry out work for each other.

○ ABC Co's overhead rates are based on estimates of cost and activity levels, rather than actual amounts.

○ ABC Co wishes to avoid under or over absorption of overheads in its production cost.

43 ABC Co absorbs fixed production overheads in one of its departments on the basis of machine hours. There were 100,000 budgeted machine hours for the forthcoming period. The fixed production overhead absorption rate was $2.50 per machine hour.

During the period, the following actual results were recorded:

Machine hours   110,000
Fixed production overheads $300,000

Which of the following statements is correct?

O   Overheads were $25,000 over-absorbed.
O   Overheads were $25,000 under-absorbed.
O   Overheads were $50,000 over-absorbed.
O   Overheads absorbed were the same as actual overheads.

---

44 A company produces a product (the ET65) in two production cost centres.

	Cost centre 1	Cost centre 2
Direct material cost per unit.	$65.00	$30.00
Direct labour hours per unit.	2	1
Direct labour rate per hour	$25.00	$15.00
Production overhead absorption rate per direct labour hour	$15.00	$15.00

General overhead costs are absorbed at a rate of 5% of production cost.

To the nearest $1, calculate the selling price of the product in order to achieve a 25% return on sales.

O $261
O $271
O $298
O $287

---

45 **Which TWO of the following are Global Management Accounting Principles?**

☐   Stewardship provides insight that is influential.
☐   Communication builds trust.
☐   Impact on value is analysed.
☐   Information is relevant.

---

46 **Which of the following statements describes flexible budgets?**

O   Budgets that include variable production costs only.

O   Budgets that, by recognising different cost behaviour patterns, are designed to change as the volume of activity changes.

O   Budgets that are for a defined period of time and only include planned revenues, expenses, assets, liabilities and cash flow.

O   Budgets that are continuously updated to reflect actual results.

47 The following extracts are available from a company's financial statements.

	20X9	20X8
	$'000	$'000
Sales	60,000	90,000
Gross profit	32,000	35,000
Net profit	21,000	18,000
Capital employed	50,000	40,000

Calculate the net profit margin percentage for both 20X9 and 20X8 to one decimal place.

20X9		*20X8*	
[ ]	%	[ ]	%

---

48 The following extracts are available from a company's financial statements.

	20X9	*20X8*
	$'000	$'000
Sales	60,000	90,000
Gross profit	32,000	35,000
Net profit	21,000	18,000
Capital employed	50,000	40,000

Calculate the return on capital employed (ROCE) percentage for both 20X9 and 20X8 to one decimal place.

20X9		*20X8*	
[ ]	%	[ ]	%

---

49 The following extracts are available from a company's financial statements.

	20X9	*20X8*
	$'000	$'000
Sales	60,000	90,000
Gross profit	32,000	35,000
Net profit	21,000	18,000
Capital employed	50,000	40,000

Calculate the asset turnover for both 20X9 and 20X8 to two decimal places.

20X9		*20X8*	
[ ]	%	[ ]	%

---

50 **Which TWO of the following statements about expected values are correct?**

- [ ] Expected values are appropriate for one-off decisions.
- [ ] Expected values are calculated using weighted averages.
- [ ] Expected values are based on probabilities which are highly reliable.
- [ ] Expected values are calculated as the sum of the probabilities multiplied by the outcomes.

51 **Which of the following are properties of a normal distribution?**

Select all that apply.

☐ It is asymmetrical.
☐ It has a mean.
☐ The area under the curve totals exactly 1.
☐ The area under half of the curve totals 2.
☐ The area to the left of μ = area to right of μ.

---

52 Jolly Co manufactures three products, TP1, TP2 and TP3. Although each product is different, they are all made using the same machine. There are 60,000 available machine hours per month.

The following standard cost information is available for the products.

	TP1 $	TP2 $	TP3 $
Direct materials	70	40	80
Direct labour:			
Machine operators ($6 per hour)	36	24	42
Fixers ($6 per hour)	48	48	56
Total variable cost	154	112	178
Selling price per unit	200	158	224
Maximum demand (units)	3,000	3,500	4,500

Fixed costs are $400,000 per period.

Calculate the deficiency in machine hours for the next month in hours.

☐ hours.

---

53 Jolly Co manufactures three products, TP1, TP2 and TP3. Although each product is different, they are all made using the same machine. There are 60,000 available machine hours per month.

The following standard cost information is available for the products.

	TP1 $	TP2 $	TP3 $
Direct materials	70	40	80
Direct labour:			
Machine operators ($6 per hour)	36	24	42
Fixers ($6 per hour)	48	48	56
Total variable cost	154	112	178
Selling price per unit	200	158	224
Maximum demand (units)	3,000	3,500	4,500

Fixed costs are $400,000 per period.

For each product, calculate the contribution per machine hour to the nearest $0.01.

Contribution per machine hour (TP1) = $ [   ]

Contribution per machine hour (TP2) = $ [   ]

Contribution per machine hour (TP2) = $ [   ]

---

54   Jolly Co manufactures three products, TP1, TP2 and TP3. Although each product is different, they are all made using the same machine. There are 60,000 available machine hours per month.

The following standard cost information is available for the products.

	TP1	TP2	TP3
	$	$	$
Direct materials	70	40	80
Direct labour:			
Machine operators ($6 per hour)	48	32	56
Fixers ($6 per hour)	36	40	42
Total variable cost	154	112	178
Selling price per unit	200	158	224
Maximum demand (units)	3,000	2,500	5,000

Fixed costs are $400,000 per period.

The company has identified that the optimum production plan requires the production of 3,000 units of TP1.

To the nearest $, calculate the total contribution of TP1.

$ [   ]

---

55   **Which of the following statements are correct?**

1   Predetermined absorption rates cause the under or over-absorption of overhead costs.

2   Predetermined absorption rates smooth out differences in unit costs caused by abnormally high or low activity levels.

3   Predetermined absorption rates allow full production costs to be recorded before they would be if actual overhead costs and activity were used instead.

    O   1 and 2 only
    O   1 and 3 only
    O   2 and 3 only
    O   1, 2 and 3

56 A company records all of the calls that its customers make to its customer service centre. Last month, the company analysed all the calls made to it under three headings and recorded the length of time each call took.

The sample below is a list of call lengths from one hour on one day.

New customer call mins	Customer complaint call mins	Leaving customer call mins
40	20	10
35	22	5
30	18	5
20	23	12
20	10	15

In regards to new customer calls, which of the following statements is correct?

○ The median time for new customer calls is 30 mins.
○ The mode time for new customer calls is 40 mins.
○ The mean time for new customer calls is 20 mins.
○ None of the above statements are correct.

57 A company records all of the calls that its customers make to its customer service centre. Last month, the company analysed all the calls made to it under three headings and recorded the length of time each call took.

The sample below is a list of call lengths from one hour on one day.

New customer call mins	Customer complaint call mins	Leaving customer call mins
40	10	10
35	22	5
30	18	5
20	23	12
20	10	15

In regards to customer complaint calls, which of the following statements is correct?

○ The median time for customer complaint calls is 17 mins.
○ The mode time for customer complaint calls is 10 mins.
○ The mean time for customer complaint calls is 18 mins.
○ None of the above statements are correct.

58 A company records all of the calls that its customers make to its customer service centre. Last month, the company analysed all the calls made to it under three headings and recorded the length of time each call took. The sample below is a list of call lengths from one hour on one day.

New customer call mins	Customer complaint call mins	Leaving customer call mins
40	20	10
35	22	6
30	18	6
20	23	13
20	10	15

Calculate the mean time for leaving customer calls.

[   ]

59   **Which of the following statements describes a principal budget factor?**

○   A principal budget factor is the amount of budgetary slack added to a budget to protect against adverse variances.

○   A principal budget factor is the product of consolidating subsidiary budgets.

○   A principal budget factor is the budgeted revenue expected for the next financial period.

○   A principal budget factor is a limit on the organisation's activities.

60   **Which FOUR of the following are qualities of good information?**

☐   Authoritative
☐   Complete
☐   Cost-beneficial
☐   User targeted
☐   Error free
☐   Easy to read

Mock exam answers

1   The correct answer is: Between 15% and 20%

	$
Investment	(30,000)
PV of cash inflow	32,200
NPV @ 15%	2,200

	$
Investment	(30,000)
PV of cash inflow	29,400
NPV @ 20%	(600)

The IRR of the machine investment is therefore between 15% and 20% because the NPV falls from $2,200 at 15% to -$600 at 20%. Therefore at some point between 15% and 20% the NPV = 0. When the NPV = 0, the internal rate of return is reached.

---

2   The correct answer is: $2,725.

The expenditure variance is the difference between the flexed budget and the actual results.

Expenditure variance   = $629,105 – $631,830
                       = $2,725 (A)

---

3   The correct answer is: $3.83.

	$
Actual overheads	232,725
Under-absorbed overheads	(12,500)
Overheads absorbed by 57,500 hours	220,225
Overhead absorption rate	$220,225/57,500
	= $3.83 per machine hour

---

4   The correct answer is: An hour used to measure the total amount of output that is achievable in the time, when working at standard efficiency levels.

A standard hour is the quantity of output achievable, at standard performance, in an hour. It is often used to measure total output when dissimilar units are made.

The situation where no exceptional events occur describes ideal operating conditions, and an hour where only identical units are made describes a typical situation for many organisations that are involved in mass production.

---

5   The correct answer is: An error in calculating the standard price of direct material that resulted in a figure which is too high.

A favourable variance occurs when the price paid is less than budgeted and this would occur when the standard price is set too high.

Adverse variances occur where the price paid is greater than budget. This would occur where the material is more expensive due to higher quality and where the price increased due to loss of discount. The purchase of more material than budgeted could lead to a favourable price variance if bulk discounts were received, but this is not stated in the question.

6   The correct answer is: 0.40.

We can calculate the required probability by using the values calculated in the following contingency table.

	Pay	Default	Total
Check	40	10	50
No check	35	15	50
Total	75	25	100

Workings

No check	=	50% of 100
	=	50
Check	=	100 – 50
	=	50
No check but pay	=	70% of 50
	=	35
Check, pay	=	80% of 50
	=	40

The other figures are balancing figures. P(customer checked-defaults) = 10/25 = 0.40

---

7   The correct answer is: 1 and 2 only

In service costing it is difficult to identify many attributable direct costs. Many costs must be shared over several cost units, therefore characteristic 1 does apply. Composite cost units such as tonne-mile or room-night are often used, therefore characteristic 2 does apply. Tangible means 'touchable', such as a physical unit like a laptop, therefore characteristic 3 does not apply.

---

8   The correct answers are:

- Avoidable costs
- Opportunity costs
- Differential costs

Avoidable costs are relevant because they are affected by the decision, eg we are currently paying rent and if we were to buy or build our own workplace, this rent would become a cost saving (avoidable cost/relevant cost).

If there are any future costs incurred due to a decision we make, then they come under relevant costs of the decision. However, future committed costs are irrelevant. For example, the salary of a new supervisor recruited specifically for the new building is a future relevant cost. However, if we were to recruit a new supervisor to start in six months' time (future) and we were to use them in the new project then their salary becomes irrelevant because it is a future committed cost.

Opportunity costs are the next best alternatives forgone due to the decision we make so we must consider them as relevant. For example, a management accountant who is currently an employee, giving up their job to start up their own business. The salary is an opportunity cost in this decision.

Differential costs are another name for incremental costs (eg at the moment we are paying a rent of $6,000 but if we had to pay rent of $8,500, the differential cost of $2,500 is relevant to the decision of expanding).

---

9   The correct answer is: $88.57.

	$ per unit
Material	12.50
Labour	28.60
Production overhead (3 hrs × $5.50)	16.50
Total production cost	57.60
General overhead (15% × $57.50)	8.64
Total cost	66.24
Required return from product per unit ($1,674,750 × 0.20)/15,000	22.33
Required selling price	88.57

10   The correct answer is: Under absorbed by $8,579

Budgeted overhead absorption rate $\dfrac{\$641,300}{14,575}$ = $44 per labour hour

	$
Overhead absorbed = $44 × 14,359 hours	631,796
Overhead incurred	640,375
Under absorbed overhead	8,579

If you selected the second or third options you calculated the difference between the budgeted and actual overheads and interpreted the result as an under or over absorption.

If you selected the fourth option your calculations were correct but you misinterpreted the result as over absorbed.

11   The correct answer is: $145,000.

Contribution for 20,000 units:

	$'000
Sales revenue	275
Direct material	(55)
Direct labour	(40)
Variable overhead	(30)
	150

	$
∴ contribution for 24,000 units = 150 × 1.2 =	180,000
Less fixed costs	35,000
Flexed budget profit for 24,000 units	145,000

12   The correct answer is: A standard that is kept unchanged, to show the trend in costs.

A basic standard is established for use over a long period and is used to show trends. The other options describe ideal, attainable, and current standards respectively.

13   The correct answer is: Actual manufacturing overheads.

The actual material and labour costs for a batch can be determined from the material and labour recording system. Actual manufacturing overheads cannot be determined for a specific batch because of the need for allocation and apportionment of each item of overhead expenditure, and the subsequent calculation of a predetermined overhead absorption rate.

14   The correct answer is: 5%.

Coefficient of variation   =   standard deviation/mean
                            =   0.5/10
                            =   0.05
                            =   5%

15   The correct answers are:

- Payback is a fairly easy technique to understand.
- Payback ignores the time value of money.

A benefit of payback is that it is a simple technique to understand, but a disadvantage is that it ignores the time value of money.

The other options are incorrect, payback only takes account of the cash flows up to the point of payback and it can be used for projects of any life.

16   The correct answers are:

- Someone subject to oversight by a body with disciplinary powers.

- Someone committed to the values of accuracy, honesty, integrity, objectivity, transparency and reliability.

- Someone with skills, knowledge and expertise tested by examination and continuously developed in a structured and monitored context.

These are the three standards of a 'professional' according to IFAC's definition. Professionals are often bound by ethical rules or frameworks but this is not part of IFAC's definition.

17   The correct answer is: To operate at a certain level of efficiency.

The three objectives of not-for-profit organisations such as public services are, value for money, efficiency and effectiveness.

18   The correct answer is: $8,000

	Units	$
High output	2,200	47,600
Low output	1,500	35,000
	700	12,600

Variable cost per unit $12,600/700   = $18 per unit.

Fixed costs   = $35,000 – ($18 × 1,500)

    = $8,000

The second option is the total cost for an activity of 700 units: ($18 × 700) + $8,000 = $20,600.

The third option is the total variable cost for 700 units (700 × $18).

The fourth option is the total variable cost for 1,500 units (1,500 × $18).

---

19   The correct answer is: 216,250

		$	$
Sales	(52,500 × $24)		1,260,000
Direct materials	(57,500 × $4.25)	244,375	
Direct labour	(57,500 × $3.50)	201,250	
Variable overhead	(57,500 × $1.75)	100,625	
Less closing	(5,000 × $9.50)	(47,500)	
Inventory			498,750
Contribution			761,250
Less fixed costs			545,000
Profit			216,250

---

20   The correct answer is: $263,750

		$	$
Sales	(52,500 × $24)		1,260,000
Materials	(57,500 × $4.25)	244,375	
Direct labour	(57,500 × $3.50)	201,250	
Variable overhead	(57,500 × $1.75)	100,625	
Fixed costs	(57,500 × $9.50)	546,250	
Less closing inventory	(5,000 × $19)		(95,000)
			997,500
Over-absorbed overhead (W)			1,250
Absorption costing profit			263,750

Workings

Overhead absorbed	(57,500 × $9.50)	546,250
Overhead incurred		545,000
Over-absorbed overhead		1,250

21 The correct answer is: Profit under absorption costing was higher than under marginal costing by $47,500.

Closing inventory at the end of the month is 5,000 units (57,500 − 52,500) which is higher than the opening inventory (zero). This means that absorption costing will report a higher profit than marginal costing.

Difference in profit = OAR × difference in inventory units
                      = $9.50 × 5,000 units
                      = $47,500

22 The correct answer is: $40,000

The value of the perpetuity is calculated as: 2,000/0.05 = 40,000

23 The correct answer is: Externality

The three E's are effectiveness, economy and efficiency.

24 The correct answer is: $1.58.

Required liquid input = 1 litres × $\dfrac{100}{95}$ = 1.05 litres

Standard cost of liquid input = 1.05 × $1.50 = $1.58 (to the nearest cent)

25 The correct answer is: Distance C.

Above the breakeven point, contribution = fixed costs + profit, therefore distance C indicates the contribution at level of activity L.

Distance A indicates the profit at level of activity L, B indicates the fixed costs and D indicates the margin of safety.

26 The correct answer is: An employee's bonus of $5 per unit for every unit above 100 units.

The total cost of the bonus is zero until activity reaches the point at which it is paid. The other options would all have some value for cost at lower activity levels.

27 The correct answer is: $95,263

Number of employees in assembly department	=	15 direct + 12 indirect
	=	27
Number of employees in all production departments	=	34 direct + 19 indirect
	=	53
Assembly department overhead		
Canteen cost apportioned to assembly department	=	$\dfrac{\$12,000}{53} \times 27$
	=	$6,113
Original overhead allocated and apportioned	=	$89,150
Total overhead after apportionment of canteen costs	=	$95,263

If you selected the first option you forgot to include the original overhead allocated and apportioned to the assembly department. If you selected the second option you included the eight canteen employees in your calculation, but the question states that the basis for apportionment is the number of employees in each production cost centre.

If you selected the third option you based your calculations on the direct employees only.

---

28   The correct answer is: $93,750.

	Litres
Opening inventory	(10,500)
Closing inventory	4,250
Change in inventory	(6,250)
x Overhead full rate	$5
Profit difference	$31,250

Since inventories reduced during the period the absorption costing profit would be lower than the marginal costing profit.

Absorption costing profit   = $125,000 – $31,250
                             = $93,750.

---

29   The correct answer is: Contact the bank to arrange an overdraft.

Arranging an overdraft is appropriate as it is intended as a temporary measure to provide protection against cash shortages.

Demanding early repayment from customers is not appropriate as it may cause them to take their business elsewhere. Paying suppliers early and increasing production will increase demand for cash and make the situation worse.

---

30   The correct answer is: Attainable standards are attained if production is carried out efficiently and machines and materials are used properly. Allowances are made for waste and inefficiencies.

A standard that can be attained if production is carried out efficiently, machines are operated properly and/or materials are used properly. Some allowance is made for waste and inefficiencies.

Attainable standards may provide an incentive for employees to work harder as they represent a realistic but challenging target of efficiency.

A standard which is based on currently attainable working conditions describes a current standard. Current standards do not attempt to improve current levels of efficiency.

A standard which is established for use over a long period and which is used to show trends describes a basic standard. Basic standards are not particularly useful for control nor for motivating employees.

A standard which can be attained under perfect operating conditions, and which does not include an allowance for wastage, spoilage, machine breakdowns and other inefficiencies describes an ideal standard. Ideal standards are not very useful for day-to-day control and they can demotivate employees because they are highly unlikely to be achieved.

BPP
LEARNING
MEDIA

31   The correct answer is: $5.60.

Workings

Sales are 60,000 units at the normal level of activity. Variable costs at 60,000 units of production/sales are as follows.

	$	$ per unit
Production overhead	30,000	0.50
Sales costs (5% of $600,000)	30,000	0.50
Distribution costs	15,000	0.25
Administration overhead	9,000	0.15
	84,000	1.40
Direct costs	180,000	3.00
Total variable costs	264,000	4.40
Sales revenue	600,000	10.00
Contribution	336,000	5.60

32   The correct answer is: $252,000

The fixed cost per month is $252,000.

Fixed costs	$
Production overhead	126,000
Sales costs	50,000
Distribution costs	45,000
Administration overhead	31,000
	252,000

33   The correct answer is: 45,000 units.

The breakeven volume of sales per month is 45,000 units.

$$\text{Breakeven point} = \frac{\text{Fixed costs}}{\text{Contribution per unit}}$$

$$= \frac{\$252,000}{\$5.60}$$

$$= 45,000 \text{ units}$$

34   The correct answers are:

- Sales budget
- Material cost budget
- Advertising budget

A functional budget is a budget prepared for a particular function or department.

The sales, material cost budget and advertising budgets are all prepared for specific functions, therefore they are functional budgets.

35 The correct answer is: $250 (A)

10,000 litres should have cost (× $0.40)	$4,000
But did cost	$4,250
Direct material price variance	$250 (A)

If you selected the first or second options you based your calculations on the materials issued to production. However, the material inventory account is maintained at standard cost; therefore the material price variance is calculated when the materials are purchased. If you selected the fourth option you calculated the size of the variance correctly but you misinterpreted it as favourable.

---

36 The correct answers are:

- Where production of the product lasts for a relatively short time.
- Where production is for a single special order.

Job costing is appropriate where each cost unit is separately identifiable (such as a special job) and is of relatively short duration. It is not designed for use over long periods such as over several accounting periods or continuously.

---

37 The correct answer is: $41,700

Present value = $10,000 + (10,000 × 3.170) = $41,700

---

38 The correct answer is: Initial investment ÷ annual net cash inflow.

The payback period is the time that is required for the total of the cash inflows of a capital investment project to equal the total of the cash outflows, ie initial investment ÷ annual net cash inflow.

---

39 The correct answer is: $15,920

($35,000 × 3.312) − $100,000 = $15,920.

---

40 The correct answers are:

	(i) Strategic-level information	(ii) Operational-level information
Forward looking	☑	☐
Historical	☐	☑
Externally focused	☑	☐
Internally focused	☐	☑
Relevant to the long-term	☑	☐
Relevant to the short-term	☐	☑

Strategic-level information is: used by senior managers, unstructured, forward-looking and externally focused, qualitative and quantitative, relevant to long term, highly summarised, uses estimates, derived from internal and external sources, uses a wide variety of information and formats.

Operational-level information is: used by front line managers, detailed, structured, numerical and internally focused on the decision, relevant to immediate term, derived almost entirely from historical and internal sources.

41   The correct answer is: Mixed cost

The depicted cost has a basic fixed element, which is payable even at zero activity, and a variable element that is added at a constant rate as activity increases.

42   The correct answer is: ABC Co's service departments carry out work for each other.

There are several ways of reapportioning service department overheads to production departments. The repeated distribution method recognises inter- service department work, therefore the correct answer is 'ABC Co's service departments carry out work for each other'. The other options might be correct, but there could be other reasons behind them.

43   Correct answer is: Overheads were $25,000 under-absorbed.

Overhead was $25,000 under-absorbed.

Budget hrs	100,000
Standard hrs	110,000
Difference	10,000 × $2.50 =$25,000

44   The correct answer is: $287

	Cost centre 1	Cost centre 2	Total
	$ per unit	$ per unit	$ per unit
Direct material	65.00	30.00	95.00
Direct labour	50.00	15.00	65.00
Production overhead	30.00	15.00	45.00
Total production cost			205.00
General overhead cost at 5%			10.25
			215.25
Profit margin (× 25/75)			71.75
Required selling price per unit			287.00

45   The correct answers are:

- Impact on value is analysed.
- Information is relevant.

The Global Management Accounting Principles were created by the AICPA (American Institute of CPAs) and CIMA. They are:

- Stewardship builds trust.
- Communication provides insight that is influential.
- Impact on value is analysed.
- Information is relevant.

46 The correct answer is: Budgets that, by recognising different cost behaviour patterns, are designed to change as the volume of activity changes.

A flexible budget can help managers to make more valid comparisons. It is designed to show the allowed expenditure for the actual number of units produced and sold. By comparing this flexible budget with the actual expenditure, it is possible to identify genuine efficiencies as opposed to differences caused by a change in activity level.

47 The correct answer is:

	20X9	20X8
Net profit margin	21,000/60,000 = 35.0%	18,000/90,000 = 20.0%

48 The correct answer is:

	20X9	20X8
ROCE	21,000/50,000 = 42.0%	18,000/40,000 = 45.0%

49 The correct answer is:

	20X9	20X8
Asset turnover	60,000/50,000 = 120%	90,000/40,000 = 225%

50 The correct answers are:

- Expected values are calculated using weighted averages.
- Expected values are calculated as the sum of the probabilities multiplied by the outcomes.

These statements define an expected value. Expected values are not appropriate for one-off decisions and the probabilities they are based on may be unreliable. These are both limitations of expected values.

51 The correct answer is:

- It has a mean.
- The area under the curve totals exactly 1.
- The area to the left of μ = area to right of μ.

These are correct properties. The normal distribution is not asymmetrical and the area under half the curve does not total 2.

52 The correct answer is: 3,500 hours

Workings

	TP1	TP2	TP3	Total
Machine hours required per unit (machine operators cost /$6)	6	4	7	
Maximum demand (units)	3,000	2,500	5,000	
Total machine hours required	18,000	14,000	31,500	63,500
Machine hours available				60,000
Deficiency in machine hours for next period				3,500

53 The correct answers are:

Contribution per machine hour (TP1) = $7.67.

Contribution per machine hour (TP2) = $11.50.

Contribution per machine hour (TP3) = $6.57.

Workings

	TP1	TP2	TP3
	$	$	$
Selling price per unit	200	158	224
Variable cost per unit	154	112	178
Contribution per unit	46	46	46
Machine hours per unit	6	4	7
Contribution per machine hour	$7.67	$11.50	$6.57

54 The correct answer is: $138,000

3,000 × $46 = $138,000

55 The correct answer is: 1, 2 and 3

Statement 1 is correct because a constant unit absorption rate is used throughout the period.

Statement 2 is correct because 'actual' overhead costs, based on actual overhead expenditure and actual activity for the period, cannot be determined until after the end of the period.

Statement 3 is correct because the method predetermines an activity level which may differ from what actually happens.

56 The correct answer is: The median time for new customer calls is 30 mins.

We need to put the numbers in order and find the middle value. As there are 5 numbers, the middle value will be the 3rd number. 20, 20, 30, 35, 40

The 3rd number is 30.

The mode time is the most common time and this is 20 which occurs twice.

To calculate the mean time we add up all of the times and divide by the number of results (ie 5). (40 + 35 + 30 + 20 + 20)/5 = 50/5 = 29.

57 The correct answer is: The mode time for customer complaint calls is 10 mins.

The mode is the most common time, ie 10, as it occurs twice in the list.

To find the median time we need to put the numbers in order and find the middle value. As there are 5 numbers, the middle value will be the 3rd number. 10, 10, 18, 22, 23

The 3rd number is 18.

To calculate the mean time we add up all of the times and divide by the number of results (ie 5). (10 + 22 + 18 + 23 + 10)/5 = 50/5 = 16.6.

58   The correct answer is: 10.

We add up all of the times and divide by the number of results (ie 5). 10 + 6 + 6 + 13 + 15)/5 = 50/5 = 10.

59   The correct answer is: A principal budget factor is a limit on the organisation's activities

The principal budget factor can also be known as the limiting factor as this factor usually indicates which budget should be prepared first. Failure to identify the principal budgeting factor at an early stage could lead to delays at a later stage when managers realise targets that were set are not feasible.

60   The correct answers are:

- Authoritative
- Complete
- Cost-beneficial
- User targeted

Good information should be as simple as possible – remember the mnemonic ACCURATE. Accurate, Complete, Cost-beneficial, User-targeted, Relevant, Authoritative, Timely, Easy to use.

Good information should be accurate – but this is no guarantee that it is completely free from error. Just because information is easy to read does not mean that it is good.

LINEAR REGRESSION

The linear regression equation of Y on X is given by:

$$Y = a + bX \text{ or } Y - \overline{Y} = b(X - \overline{X})$$

where

$$b = \frac{Covariance(XY)}{Variance(X)} = \frac{n\sum XY - (\sum X)(\sum Y)}{n\sum X^2 - (\sum X)^2}$$

and

$$a = \overline{Y} - b\overline{X}$$

PRESENT VALUE TABLE

Present value of 1.00 unit of currency, that is $(1+r)^{-n}$ where r = interest rate; n = number of periods until payment or receipt.

Periods (n)	Interest rates (r)									
	1%	2%	3%	4%	5%	6%	7%	8%	9%	10%
1	0.990	0.980	0.971	0.962	0.952	0.943	0.935	0.926	0.917	0.909
2	0.980	0.961	0.943	0.925	0.907	0.890	0.873	0.857	0.842	0.826
3	0.971	0.942	0.915	0.889	0.864	0.840	0.816	0.794	0.772	0.751
4	0.961	0.924	0.888	0.855	0.823	0.792	0.763	0.735	0.708	0.683
5	0.951	0.906	0.863	0.822	0.784	0.747	0.713	0.681	0.650	0.621
6	0.942	0.888	0.837	0.790	0.746	0.705	0.666	0.630	0.596	0.564
7	0.933	0.871	0.813	0.760	0.711	0.665	0.623	0.583	0.547	0.513
8	0.923	0.853	0.789	0.731	0.677	0.627	0.582	0.540	0.502	0.467
9	0.914	0.837	0.766	0.703	0.645	0.592	0.544	0.500	0.460	0.424
10	0.905	0.820	0.744	0.676	0.614	0.558	0.508	0.463	0.422	0.386
11	0.896	0.804	0.722	0.650	0.585	0.527	0.475	0.429	0.388	0.350
12	0.887	0.788	0.701	0.625	0.557	0.497	0.444	0.397	0.356	0.319
13	0.879	0.773	0.681	0.601	0.530	0.469	0.415	0.368	0.326	0.290
14	0.870	0.758	0.661	0.577	0.505	0.442	0.388	0.340	0.299	0.263
15	0.861	0.743	0.642	0.555	0.481	0.417	0.362	0.315	0.275	0.239
16	0.853	0.728	0.623	0.534	0.458	0.394	0.339	0.292	0.252	0.218
17	0.844	0.714	0.605	0.513	0.436	0.371	0.317	0.270	0.231	0.198
18	0.836	0.700	0.587	0.494	0.416	0.350	0.296	0.250	0.212	0.180
19	0.828	0.686	0.570	0.475	0.396	0.331	0.277	0.232	0.194	0.164
20	0.820	0.673	0.554	0.456	0.377	0.312	0.258	0.215	0.178	0.149

Periods (n)	Interest rates (r)									
	11%	12%	13%	14%	15%	16%	17%	18%	19%	20%
1	0.901	0.893	0.885	0.877	0.870	0.862	0.855	0.847	0.840	0.833
2	0.812	0.797	0.783	0.769	0.756	0.743	0.731	0.718	0.706	0.694
3	0.731	0.712	0.693	0.675	0.658	0.641	0.624	0.609	0.593	0.579
4	0.659	0.636	0.613	0.592	0.572	0.552	0.534	0.516	0.499	0.482
5	0.593	0.567	0.543	0.519	0.497	0.476	0.456	0.437	0.419	0.402
6	0.535	0.507	0.480	0.456	0.432	0.410	0.390	0.370	0.352	0.335
7	0.482	0.452	0.425	0.400	0.376	0.354	0.333	0.314	0.296	0.279
8	0.434	0.404	0.376	0.351	0.327	0.305	0.285	0.266	0.249	0.233
9	0.391	0.361	0.333	0.308	0.284	0.263	0.243	0.225	0.209	0.194
10	0.352	0.322	0.295	0.270	0.247	0.227	0.208	0.191	0.176	0.162
11	0.317	0.287	0.261	0.237	0.215	0.195	0.178	0.162	0.148	0.135
12	0.286	0.257	0.231	0.208	0.187	0.168	0.152	0.137	0.124	0.112
13	0.258	0.229	0.204	0.182	0.163	0.145	0.130	0.116	0.104	0.093
14	0.232	0.205	0.181	0.160	0.141	0.125	0.111	0.099	0.088	0.078
15	0.209	0.183	0.160	0.140	0.123	0.108	0.095	0.084	0.074	0.065
16	0.188	0.163	0.141	0.123	0.107	0.093	0.081	0.071	0.062	0.054
17	0.170	0.146	0.125	0.108	0.093	0.080	0.069	0.060	0.052	0.045
18	0.153	0.130	0.111	0.095	0.081	0.069	0.059	0.051	0.044	0.038
19	0.138	0.116	0.098	0.083	0.070	0.060	0.051	0.043	0.037	0.031
20	0.124	0.104	0.087	0.073	0.061	0.051	0.043	0.037	0.031	0.026

BPP LEARNING MEDIA

Cumulative present value of 1.00 unit of currency per annum, Receivable or Payable at the end of each year for n years $\frac{1-(1+r)^{-n}}{r}$

Periods	Interest rates (r)									
(n)	1%	2%	3%	4%	5%	6%	7%	8%	9%	10%
1	0.990	0.980	0.971	0.962	0.952	0.943	0.935	0.926	0.917	0.909
2	1.970	1.942	1.913	1.886	1.859	1.833	1.808	1.783	1.759	1.736
3	2.941	2.884	2.829	2.775	2.723	2.673	2.624	2.577	2.531	2.487
4	3.902	3.808	3.717	3.630	3.546	3.465	3.387	3.312	3.240	3.170
5	4.853	4.713	4.580	4.452	4.329	4.212	4.100	3.993	3.890	3.791
6	5.795	5.601	5.417	5.242	5.076	4.917	4.767	4.623	4.486	4.355
7	6.728	6.472	6.230	6.002	5.786	5.582	5.389	5.206	5.033	4.868
8	7.652	7.325	7.020	6.733	6.463	6.210	5.971	5.747	5.535	5.335
9	8.566	8.162	7.786	7.435	7.108	6.802	6.515	6.247	5.995	5.759
10	9.471	8.983	8.530	8.111	7.722	7.360	7.024	6.710	6.418	6.145
11	10.368	9.787	9.253	8.760	8.306	7.887	7.499	7.139	6.805	6.495
12	11.255	10.575	9.954	9.385	8.863	8.384	7.943	7.536	7.161	6.814
13	12.134	11.348	10.635	9.986	9.394	8.853	8.358	7.904	7.487	7.103
14	13.004	12.106	11.296	10.563	9.899	9.295	8.745	8.244	7.786	7.367
15	13.865	12.849	11.938	11.118	10.380	9.712	9.108	8.559	8.061	7.606
16	14.718	13.578	12.561	11.652	10.838	10.106	9.447	8.851	8.313	7.824
17	15.562	14.292	13.166	12.166	11.274	10.477	9.763	9.122	8.544	8.022
18	16.398	14.992	13.754	12.659	11.690	10.828	10.059	9.372	8.756	8.201
19	17.226	15.679	14.324	13.134	12.085	11.158	10.336	9.604	8.950	8.365
20	18.046	16.351	14.878	13.590	12.462	11.470	10.594	9.818	9.129	8.514

Periods	Interest rates (r)									
(n)	11%	12%	13%	14%	15%	16%	17%	18%	19%	20%
1	0.901	0.893	0.885	0.877	0.870	0.862	0.855	0.847	0.840	0.833
2	1.713	1.690	1.668	1.647	1.626	1.605	1.585	1.566	1.547	1.528
3	2.444	2.402	2.361	2.322	2.283	2.246	2.210	2.174	2.140	2.106
4	3.102	3.037	2.974	2.914	2.855	2.798	2.743	2.690	2.639	2.589
5	3.696	3.605	3.517	3.433	3.352	3.274	3.199	3.127	3.058	2.991
6	4.231	4.111	3.998	3.889	3.784	3.685	3.589	3.498	3.410	3.326
7	4.712	4.564	4.423	4.288	4.160	4.039	3.922	3.812	3.706	3.605
8	5.146	4.968	4.799	4.639	4.487	4.344	4.207	4.078	3.954	3.837
9	5.537	5.328	5.132	4.946	4.772	4.607	4.451	4.303	4.163	4.031
10	5.889	5.650	5.426	5.216	5.019	4.833	4.659	4.494	4.339	4.192
11	6.207	5.938	5.687	5.453	5.234	5.029	4.836	4.656	4.486	4.327
12	6.492	6.194	5.918	5.660	5.421	5.197	4.988	4.793	4.611	4.439
13	6.750	6.424	6.122	5.842	5.583	5.342	5.118	4.910	4.715	4.533
14	6.982	6.628	6.302	6.002	5.724	5.468	5.229	5.008	4.802	4.611
15	7.191	6.811	6.462	6.142	5.847	5.575	5.324	5.092	4.876	4.675
16	7.379	6.974	6.604	6.265	5.954	5.668	5.405	5.162	4.938	4.730
17	7.549	7.120	6.729	6.373	6.047	5.749	5.475	5.222	4.990	4.775
18	7.702	7.250	6.840	6.467	6.128	5.818	5.534	5.273	5.033	4.812
19	7.839	7.366	6.938	6.550	6.198	5.877	5.584	5.316	5.070	4.843
20	7.963	7.469	7.025	6.623	6.259	5.929	5.628	5.353	5.101	4.870

Area under the normal curve

This table gives the area under the normal curve between the mean and the point Z standard deviations above the mean. The corresponding area for deviations below the mean can be found by symmetry.

$Z = \dfrac{(x - \mu)}{\sigma}$	0.00	0.01	0.02	0.03	0.04	0.05	0.06	0.07	0.08	0.09
0.0	.0000	.0040	.0080	.0120	.0160	.0199	.0239	.0279	.0319	.0359
0.1	.0398	.0438	.0478	.0517	.0557	.0596	.0636	.0675	.0714	.0753
0.2	.0793	.0832	.0871	.0910	.0948	.0987	.1026	.1064	.1103	.1141
0.3	.1179	.1217	.1255	.1293	.1331	.1368	.1406	.1443	.1480	.1517
0.4	.1554	.1591	.1628	.1664	.1700	.1736	.1772	.1808	.1844	.1879
0.5	.1915	.1950	.1985	.2019	.2054	.2088	.2123	.2157	.2190	.2224
0.6	.2257	.2291	.2324	.2357	.2389	.2422	.2454	.2486	.2517	.2549
0.7	.2580	.2611	.2642	.2673	.2704	.2734	.2764	.2794	.2823	.2852
0.8	.2881	.2910	.2939	.2967	.2995	.3023	.3051	.3078	.3106	.3133
0.9	.3159	.3186	.3212	.3238	.3264	.3289	.3315	.3340	.3365	.3389
1.0	.3413	.3438	.3461	.3485	.3508	.3531	.3554	.3577	.3599	.3621
1.1	.3643	.3665	.3686	.3708	.3729	.3749	.3770	.3790	.3810	.3830
1.2	.3849	.3869	.3888	.3907	.3925	.3944	.3962	.3980	.3997	.4015
1.3	.4032	.4049	.4066	.4082	.4099	.4115	.4131	.4147	.4162	.4177
1.4	.4192	.4207	.4222	.4236	.4251	.4265	.4279	.4292	.4306	.4319
1.5	.4332	.4345	.4357	.4370	.4382	.4394	.4406	.4418	.4429	.4441
1.6	.4452	.4463	.4474	.4484	.4495	.4505	.4515	.4525	.4535	.4545
1.7	.4554	.4564	.4573	.4582	.4591	.4599	.4608	.4616	.4625	.4633
1.8	.4641	.4649	.4656	.4664	.4671	.4678	.4686	.4693	.4699	.4706
1.9	.4713	.4719	.4726	.4732	.4738	.4744	.4750	.4756	.4761	.4767
2.0	.4772	.4778	.4783	.4788	.4793	.4798	.4803	.4808	.4812	.4817
2.1	.4821	.4826	.4830	.4834	.4838	.4842	.4846	.4850	.4854	.4857
2.2	.4861	.4864	.4868	.4871	.4875	.4878	.4881	.4884	.4887	.4890
2.3	.4893	.4896	.4898	.4901	.4904	.4906	.4909	.4911	.4913	.4916
2.4	.4918	.4920	.4922	.4925	.4927	.4929	.4931	.4932	.4934	.4936
2.5	.4938	.4940	.4941	.4943	.4945	.4946	.4948	.4949	.4951	.4952
2.6	.4953	.4955	.4956	.4957	.4959	.4960	.4961	.4962	.4963	.4964
2.7	.4965	.4966	.4967	.4968	.4969	.4970	.4971	.4972	.4973	.4974
2.8	.4974	.4975	.4976	.4977	.4977	.4978	.4979	.4979	.4980	.4981
2.9	.4981	.4982	.4982	.4983	.4984	.4984	.4985	.4985	.4986	.4986
3.0	.49865	.4987	.4987	.4988	.4988	.4989	.4989	.4989	.4990	.4990
3.1	.49903	.4991	.4991	.4991	.4992	.4992	.4992	.4992	.4993	.4993
3.2	.49931	.4993	.4994	.4994	.4994	.4994	.4994	.4995	.4995	.4995
3.3	.49952	.4995	.4995	.4996	.4996	.4996	.4996	.4996	.4996	.4997
3.4	.49966	.4997	.4997	.4997	.4997	.4997	.4997	.4997	.4997	.4998